Ambling and Scrambling on the Appalachian TRAIL

By James M. & Hertha E. Flack

APPALACHIAN TRAIL CONFERENCE
Harpers Ferry, West Virginia

Library of Congress Cataloging in Publication Data
Flack, James M., 1913-
    Ambling and scrambling on the Appalachian Trail.

    1. Hiking—Appalachian Mountains. 2. Appalachian Trail.
I. Flack, Hertha E., 1916-
II. Title.
GV199.42.A68F55   796.5'22'0974   81-51172
                                                         AACR2

Photo Credit: James M. Flack

*We dedicate this book
to our late and beloved friend, George Dusenbury*

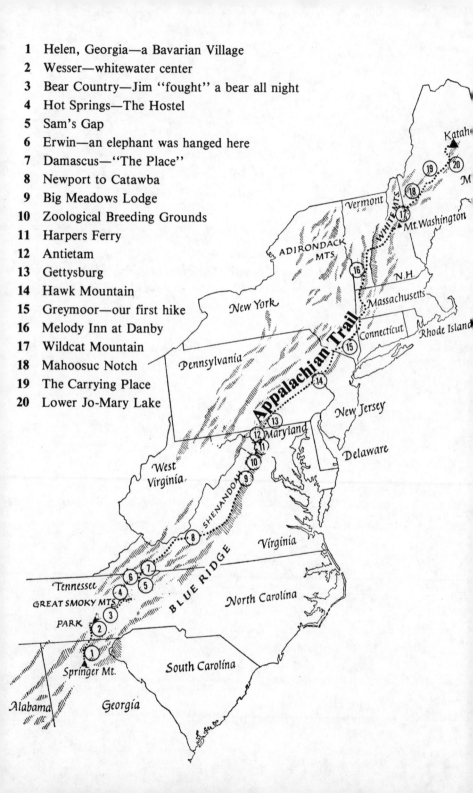

1 Helen, Georgia—a Bavarian Village
2 Wesser—whitewater center
3 Bear Country—Jim "fought" a bear all night
4 Hot Springs—The Hostel
5 Sam's Gap
6 Erwin—an elephant was hanged here
7 Damascus—"The Place"
8 Newport to Catawba
9 Big Meadows Lodge
10 Zoological Breeding Grounds
11 Harpers Ferry
12 Antietam
13 Gettysburg
14 Hawk Mountain
15 Greymoor—our first hike
16 Melody Inn at Danby
17 Wildcat Mountain
18 Mahoosuc Notch
19 The Carrying Place
20 Lower Jo-Mary Lake

Contents

Ambling

Preface

Before storing our Appalachian Trail guidebooks, notes and copies of travel letters, we decided that our friends and family were entitled to an organized statement or report about what we have really been doing out in the woods. Well, here it is. We may not have told it all, perhaps, but to the best of our ability we have set forth the essence of our walk between Springer Mountain in Georgia and Katahdin in Maine.

I am responsible for the narrative. It is based upon notes recorded on maps or in guidebooks and upon shared memories. Tah (short for Hertha) with her customary flair has captured and recorded in her letters home the feel and color of the highlights of our eight months of walking over eight years.

Our friends have been most patient. I am sure they will have mixed feelings when we say that with this manuscript we put this adventure behind us—so that we can get on with the next one!

We owe thanks to all members of our family and to supporting friends who have helped us in many ways. We especially want to thank Karen Bonnell, our daughter, for worrying about us, acting as clearinghouse for messages, for shuttle services. Karen and her husband, Tom, along with their children, Charlie and Jennifer, provided a lovely oasis as a rest-stop for recovery and doing the laundry. Our son, Jim, and his wife, Betsy, have encouraged us by their suggestions and their example of living the outdoor life. Bob and his wife, Lucy, with their two children, Betsy and Jesse, have supported us with shuttle service and their good company. Suzanne, our youngest, hiked with us in the Smokies during a "moment of truth." We give our special thanks to Azalea Cannon, our friend and helper year in and year out. She has helped us pack and unpack before and after our many trips to the Trail. And she has faithfully "baby-sat" our house and belongings so that we could hike with peace of mind.

Special friends gave us special help and "kept us company." Betty and Norme Frost, our neighbors on Wilderness Road in Tryon, North Carolina, provided shuttle service and hiked portions of the Trail with us in the Great Smokies and in the Cherokee National Forest in Tennessee. Marie Louise (M.L.) Woody and Gladys Culberson, two members of Tah's bridge group, drove with us and helped shuttle our car at Allen Gap and Devil Fork Gap. Ben and Sally Drew of Vershire, Vermont shuttled for us frequently, and they also hiked many sections with us in Vermont and New Hampshire.

We wish to thank employees of the Appalachian Trail Conference headquarters in Harpers Ferry, West Virginia for their enthusiasm and support for the future of the Appalachian Trail and for their encouragement to us to proceed on this manuscript; to Jean Cashin, the hikers' best friend at the front desk at ATC headquarters. She always made our least request seem important. We greatly appreciate the support of Col. Lester L. Holmes, former Executive Director of the ATC. He read an early copy of this manuscript and made many helpful suggestions. We also wish to thank Jean Boutilier, our friend and amanuensis without peer. She typed and retyped our notes and dictation.

And with broken hearts, we extend loving condolences to the family of George Dusenbury, the designer of this book, who recently died as the result of a tragic gas explosion in his cellar. George provided much of the professionalism detectable between these covers. We thank you, George. We feel that you became a part of us and of the Trail.

We were uncommonly fortunate that George's son, George A. Dusenbury III of Chapel Hill, North Carolina was eminently qualified and desirous of carrying on what his father had begun. So, with the competent assistance of Vicky Smith, his associate, young George saw us through the design phase of this volume.

Claudia Kravets provided her assistance in preparing the manuscript for typesetting.

And finally we are particularly indebted to Rita Malone, former Director of Publications for the Appalachian Trail Conference, for her patience and skills, both of which she extended to us most graciously. As the major editor of this publication she worked tirelessly to pull together the diverse pieces of material, and she shepherded the publication through to its final production.

We present this little volume to you with as much humility as two very proud people can muster.

James M. Flack
Tryon, North Carolina

. . . and Scrambling

What we did and why we did it

We grandparents look pretty happy as we finish the last of the 2100-plus miles that make up the Appalachian Trail, don't we? Well, I think Tah and I had every right to.

We had walked our last mile of the Trail, counting down, out loud, each tenth of a mile to the finish. At eleven a.m. Thursday, September 28, 1978, we emerged from the woods at Black Rock Gap, Shenandoah National Park, Virginia to complete our last segment of the 2,100-mile foot-trail between Katahdin, Maine and Springer Mountain, Georgia. Joy of achievement was never sweeter! "We did it! We did it!" we said again and again.

With the joy of accomplishment, there was an intermingled feeling of regret that it was over. No, we did not want to start over and do it again. It was more a feeling of loss of a desirable discipline, a schedule to keep, a task to perform—a pleasurable discipline and task. We figured that the missing discipline would be replaced by another. Meanwhile, we cherish the memories of our extended walks.

During the course of hiking the Trail, we permitted (even sought) many interruptions. We had no desire to do the whole thing in one year. Indeed, for the first two or three years, our purpose was not even to hike the whole Trail; it was simply to escape from New York City for recreation on weekends and vacations, and then only in the spring and fall.

As my schedule of going to the office reduced, our schedule of hiking increased. And, finally, after full retirement on December 31, 1974, hiking became our principal form of recreation. I gave up golf and tennis, except for an occasional nine-hole round of golf with Tah in the late afternoon as a quickie way of getting walking exercise. We continued to ski in the winter, scheduling at least one trip a year to Alta, Utah or to Austria. During hot summer months, we backpacked into the Canadian Rockies, the Austrian Alps or the Rondane National Park in Norway, where summer temperatures are moderate.

It is customary for through-hikers of the Trail to start at the southern terminus at Springer Mountain and hike north with the spring to Katahdin. A few do it in reverse, Katahdin to Springer. Tah and I followed no set pattern. Over the years we hiked segments here, there and yonder, logging each hike in the appropriate trail guide as we completed it.

Hiking the Appalachian Trail is a major accomplishment at any stage of one's life, whether completed in one year or over several years, as in our case. Those who complete in the same year they start it are in a special category of adventurers. These are generally youths in their late teens or early twenties, just out of school or college before settling down to the next phase of life. Most have arrived at an "in-between" stage, with a sufficiently

long pause before them to make a commitment to hike five or six months. The comments in the registers at the lean-tos provide some insight into how the through-hikers feel. One fellow thanked the Trail; he was proud to have done it. It was the "greatest achievement of my life, next to graduating from high school." Several wrote to the effect that they didn't know how or why they hiked the whole Trail, but they were glad that they did it. Some expressed disdain for those who put emphasis upon "miles per day" because they "missed seeing its beauty."

Hiking the Trail probably does not add a single day to one's life, but a single day's hike adds joy to many days—several days before in anticipation, the day of the hike, and many days afterwards in review or retrospect.

It's a long, hard journey in all kinds of weather from below freezing to above 100-degree temperatures, from early spring to late fall. There can be muscle-aching, blistered-toed, insect-bitten days. Mists, fog, hail and sleet and deluges of rain test the stamina and the will-power. But even in the face of such adversities one can look through to brighter, sweeter days, days of ecstasy and

delight, days of coming to know and enjoy people of kindred spirits. Long-distance hikers are a special cut. We relished the days of meeting the wilderness creatures, greeting them, envying them and thanking the Good Lord for the privilege of being allowed to be a part of the "miracle of nature." Those who complete the Trail have a lifetime of enjoyment in reflecting upon the intimate events of the trip.

Why did we do it? Why hike all those miles in the mountains over such a long period of time? Perhaps the answer is most clearly given in the description of the results of having done it.

The Appalachian Trail is now a part of me. It's in my being—not simply as a memory; although it is a memory and a most pleasant one. It is more. Its being—its soul—and mine are intertwined. My identity, my essence, now depends to some extent upon the Trail's identity and essence. I have changed; I have become a different person by having lived an important part of my life walking the length of the Trail. I like to think that the Trail has changed, has a new dimension in its identity, because I was there. This should not be viewed as a presumptuous assertion on my part. Anyone who has hiked the length of the Trail has had a super involvement and has effectively changed it and been changed by it. For, what is the Appalachian Trail?

It is an idea, "a pathway into the study of nature."* It's a 2,100-mile, continuous path through wilderness in parks and forests, in open country, across ranges and peaks and through villages and towns. It's a series of segments of a trail maintained and supported by dozens of hiking clubs of volunteer members. It's four and one-half million people enjoying some part of it annually; it's a hundred through-hikers each year. It's acres of ferns and mayapple in Georgia, black bears and boars in the Great Smokies, rhododendrun, galax, and the Shenandoah in Virginia, a friendly welcome in Harpers Ferry, timber rattlers and rocks in Pennsylvania, porcupines and squirrels in Vermont, huts and notches in New Hampshire, and blow-downs, beavers, and bogs in Maine. It's all of these and more. But most importantly it's the people who walk it and work on it and live along it from Maine to

*Benton MacKaye, in his letter to Edward B. Garvey, March 1, 1972, reprinted in Garvey's book, "Appalachian Hiker II," Appalachian Books, 1978.

Georgia. It is now so much a part of me that I feel it, live it and respond to it continuously. It's a "pathway to the inner self."

Not only has the Trail become an integral part of me, it has become an important part of "us," Tah and me. For nearly four decades we have been bonded together, with many interests in common—like hiking, skiing, touring, marriage, four children and six grandchildren—and with many individual interests. We have maintained our separate identities while being practically one. Now we have become one-plus, because we have shared the Appalachian Trail. We, as one-plus, have become identified in our being with all who have hiked the Trail, whether one section or the entire length of it.

We celebrated our thirty-seventh wedding anniversary on the Trail one month before completing it. This was the fourth year in a row that we had celebrated this important date on the Trail, and I think that this says a lot about our relationship and our mutual interests. We are of one accord that no other activity or event has provided us with so much joy and mutual respect as hiking the Trail.

James M. Black

Moments of truth

Later, we worried that one bear had read the sign

Our first sight of the bear trap had been reassuring. If a bear turned mean, we were told, the Park Ranger would bait the trap, catch the bear, and release him far away from tenderfeet like Tah, Suzanne, and me. That night, though, we wondered about the whole thing.

It was the second night of a backpacking trip on the Appalachian Trail in the Great Smoky Mountains. Suzanne, our daughter on vacation from college, was with us. Things were quiet

that moonless June night, with brilliant stars. A light breeze blew. But it was warm inside those down sleeping bags; so we had opened them up.

At about eleven o'clock Tah reached over and shook me and whispered: "Up there! To the left!" I heard the noises of an animal cracking limbs and crushing leaves as he walked. Yes! No doubt about it; we had a visitor nearby! We stayed very quiet.

Immediately I began to have qualms about our decision to

pitch camp out on the open trail with no enclosed shelter to protect against marauding animals. The night before we had slept comfortably in the Double Springs Gap Shelter; it had twelve bunk places and a heavy wire-mesh fencing across the front to keep out the bears. Our guide book repeatedly cautioned all hikers about bears: "Don't feed them; don't leave food or food-odors about; secret food and hang it in small trees that will bend or preferably break under their bulkiness or heavy weight; give bears a wide berth if met on trails." We had felt safe and comfortable sleeping behind that mesh wire.

Our plan had been to spend the second night in a protected shelter again. However, by the time we reached the east foot of Thunderhead Mountain at five o'clock, we were in the early stages of exhaustion.

After climbing for five minutes up Thunderhead, we stopped and huddled to consider the pros and cons of continuing to Old Spence Field Shelter, across the top of Thunderhead, some two miles farther. The alternative was to camp in Beechnut Gap, five minutes to the rear, where there was a good site with a spring. Charred wood in a depression, lined with stones, indicated that others had camped there before. We had a permit to make a fire.

Earlier on the Trail we had heard the following: "The climb up Thunderhead is the hardest, worst climb in the park."

This was said by a twenty-four-year-old (hiking with his girlfriend) who had just descended, but who had a month earlier climbed the route we were taking.

"You'll find going up Thunderhead real rough; it's straight up for one-half mile; but the view on the top is worth it. We saw three bears on the other side but gave them wide berth." This was from four young, husky athletes—college seniors or graduates.

We reached a consensus to return to Beechnut Gap to pitch camp. We had plenty of daylight left; so we could be leisurely, and we were. We had a marvelous dinner, following the menu which Tah had sorted out. We had a separately packaged bag for each meal.

After dinner we proceeded to lay out the best scheme for the night; the over-riding objective was to cope with the threat of bears. Suzanne announced that she would take a stick to bed with her. She had heard our friend from home, Norme Frost, say that

12

bears don't like to be hit on the nose; so the best thing is to bust them in the nose if they bother you.

We decided to place our sleeping bags some thirty yards from the campfire where we had cooked. We collected all food, including trailsnacks, gum, raisins—every single item—coffee, sugar and salt and put it all in one bag which Suzanne placed in a stump near the spring.

We hung our backpacks from small trees. At Tah's suggestion, we wiped our hands and faces liberally with insect repellant, not for insects, but to eradicate odors of food.

I placed my flashlight and hunting knife by my sleeping bag. Suzanne discarded the suggestion about busting a sniffing bear in the nose with a stick; rather she and we agreed that the best plan was to "play dead."

We settled into our sleeping bags just off the Trail. The campfire had been extinguished. The girls fell asleep quickly. But I was restless and turned fitfully. Maybe we should have gone on. How big is the risk with no protected shelter? After all, others had camped in the very same spot before—or was the fireplace only for lunches? If a bear comes sniffing, one of the girls would surely scream; that playing dead with a bear sniffing you doesn't sound for real. If he grabs Tah or Suzanne, I'll just have to get her back somehow.

So when Tah shook me out of my fitful sleep and restless thoughts, I felt sure that a confrontation was in the offing. The animal moved towards the spring. How smart we were to have moved all food out of the camp, down to the spring!

Pretty soon, we heard the sounds of slashing, like plastic bags being ripped apart—slash, slash—crack, crack. The bear started moving up from the spring towards the camp!

We abandoned the plan of staying quiet. I jumped out of my bag. I flashed the light in the direction of the spring. We talked loudly; perhaps the noises and light would scare him away. I relit the campfire. The flashlight battery might give out and there's a saying that wild animals would not walk into a lighted camp. I surely hoped that the bears respected this, too.

While making the fire, with a candle as a starter, I held my flashlight and hunting knife in my left hand, flashing the light towards the spring as the animal kept coming nearer. Soon he was

We knew of these along the trail...

within fifty feet or so of the Trail.

By now both Tah and Suzanne, in a fairly undressed state, had joined me by the fire. Suzanne ventured that he sounded like an animal smaller than a bear. This raised my hopes and screwed up my courage enough for me to pick up one of the rocks forming the base for the fire. I heaved it towards the animal. He galloped away with heavy thumps; he sounded to me like a big bear. I felt rather fortunate that he didn't hurl the rock back at me!

We had a few minutes of silence; the girls went back to bed; I decided to keep the fire going the rest of the night. This meant scrounging for a lot of wood. That was a not-too-fetching thought to have to go out into those woods for firewood!

The silence did not last. By now it was past midnight. The bear went back to thrashing around with the plastic bags of food. Slash, thrash! Occasionally he moved closer to the Trail, thrashing as he came. Soon he got so close that I called for the girls to come close to the fire. If he charged, I wanted to have the best possible chance to cope with him. Perhaps keeping the fire between the bear and us would afford some protection.

He ignored the flash of my light and our clanging of pots and pans. It appeared that he would cross that Trail into my territory. I had staked out what I considered a fair territory—a thirty-foot circle around the fire. He could have all the rest of the Great Smoky Mountains National Park. He could even have the thirty-foot circle at dawn, but for the rest of the night it was mine! We had let

14

...had hoped to reach something like this that night.

him have all our food; we had been pretty damned generous, giving all of it to him and placing it so conveniently near the spring. That was enough! I wasn't going to give in anymore!

I flashed the light towards him again. He was so near I could see the outlines of him; couldn't tell the color; but, to me it was definitely confirmed that he was a bear, and a mighty big one. I heaved another stone at him. It hit a tree right beside him with a loud clap. He turned and ran toward the spring again. He snorted and sneezed as he went. Soon he resumed slashing around with the food.

He returned toward my territory again. The girls stood behind me and the fire. I yelled at him, "Why don't you go away!" Finally, I threw another rock at him. He snorted and sneezed, but stood his ground. Shortly, however, with a defiant snort he ambled away around one o'clock.

It was quiet again, and, as it turned out, it was quiet for the rest of the night. But I vowed to be prepared for the return of the bear.

After gathering more wood, I pulled my sleeping bag close to the fire. Fully dressed with sweater, jacket and sneakers on, I lay on top of the bag with my head on a log, my hat tilted over my eyes and my flashlight and knife at hand. I stoked the fire the rest of the night. I caught a couple of cat-naps in between stoking and doing some serious thinking.

This experience in the wilderness was a moment of truth for

15

me. What would I have done had I been alone? Would I have run? No, probably not. Would I have packed (or now pack) to climb old Thunderhead in the middle of the night? I might have alone. But that was out of the question with Tah and Suzanne present. I decided that my responsibility to them could best be handled right there in the campsite.

If the bear crossed into the camp, in a rage for whatever reason, how best to cope with him? That four-inch hunting knife really should be a secondary weapon of defense. I had already firmly decided to take only defensive action, in my territory, to avoid any temptation to go on the offensive, or beyond my territory. I decided that a burning stick might be the best first-line of defense; so I kept one, four to five feet long, sticking out of the fire for that purpose.

I mentally play-acted the possible scenes of the likely encounter between that unreasonably selfish and greedy bear and me—burning stick in one hand, knife in the other, crouched in front of the fire—or better behind the fire? No, that's where Suzanne and Tah should huddle to watch. I'd have to take my stance in front.

At one point I considered the advisability of putting on my heavy hiking boots instead of the sneakers. In the event of hand-to-hand combat it might be useful to give the bear a hard boot in the stomach as I gripped his head and lay back to use leverage to throw him over my head and shoulders, maybe into the fire.

Yes, as I confronted him, I'd speak calmly to the bear as long as he intruded: "There's no more food; you've already eaten every smidgeon we had; we're going to hike ten miles tomorrow on empty stomachs as it is, and climbing Thunderhead's tough." I'd also be talking to Tah and Suzanne to keep them calm and to give them maneuvering instructions. The one most important maneuver was to keep the fire between themselves and the bear. The worst possible thing would be to bolt away from our tight circle.

I was prepared to suffer some kind of injuries, but I hoped that I could inflict sufficient wounds on the bear to have him depart. Tah could bind my wounds while Suzanne hiked for help from the Rangers. I was glad that we had packed some adhesive tape in addition to bandaids. I could possibly incur wounds which bandaids would not cover.

With all these thoughts and more, while I tended the fire every ten minutes, the night wore on. The moon arose at three, half full. I figured that daylight should come around five o'clock. So at four-thirty, I awakened the girls to prepare to break camp and climb Thunderhead after we had cleaned up the mess around the spring made by the bear.

As day broke, I opened an emergency kit which had been stashed in the bottom of my pack. I felt sure that there would be a couple of chocolate bars, a fish hook, some matches and possibly some instant coffee. There was no coffee. The bars of candy would have to do for three of us the rest of the way.

Tah and Suzanne went down to the spring to start cleaning up the mess. I stayed for a few moments to put out the fire. Tah called out, saying a couple of things. I did not understand her first sentence but the second was loud and clear: "This place is a disaster—looks like a tornado struck!" I said, "O.K., I'll be there in a moment to help." As I was on the way to help she called out again, "Our food is intact! But this place is a disaster!"

I thought, "How could that be? We heard the bear for two hours thrashing around with our bags of food."

Surely enough, there was the food, intact in the stump as Suzanne had placed it. Also, the quart of milk, made from powder, sat undisturbed in the spring. We couldn't understand it; but we were grateful to have food and coffee. We returned to camp, restarted the fire, had a big breakfast and began packing.

When we returned to the spring to get dishwater and water to put on the fire we discovered the answer as to why the bear had not taken our food. It wasn't a bear after all; it was a wild boar, which had rooted up the whole terrain between the spring and our camp. He was doing only what comes naturally, digging up the ground for roots; he wasn't interested in human or bear foods.

There it is, a true story of my night fighting a bear. It ended happily for all, except maybe for one wild, snorting boar who must have had indigestion from being disturbed during his midnight lunch.

E*pilogue.* The climb up Thunderhead the next day was comparatively easy!

According to Park Rangers, the wild boar can be more dangerous and destructive than the black bear in the Smokies!

We meet a teller of tales

Sams Gap is a pass at 3,700 feet in the southern Appalachians in the land of the Big Bald. The AT crosses the North Carolina-Tennessee state line at Sams Gap, entering the Cherokee National Forest in Tennessee and leaving the Pisgah National Forest in North Carolina.

Hubert Metcalf, his family and his relatives live there, some on one side and some on the other side of Sams Gap, but most of them on the Tennessee side. The cemetery, where generations of

Metcalfs are buried, is on the state line and the Appalachian Trail runs alongside the cemetery fence down to the highway, cutting through the pass.

Tah and I arrived at Sams Gap at about five p.m. in early July, planning to hike the Appalachian Trail two straight days, provided we could find transportation help and, also, provided we could find a good motel or inn for a couple of nights.

We drove toward Erwin, Tennessee because the Trail Guide indicated that there we would find good motel or inn accommodations as well as good food. On our way we found Hubert, plus his father-in-law and mother-in-law, sitting in the shade, on an old porch swing, next to a country store on the highway, in the cool of the late afternoon. We explained our mission and need for someone to drive us the next morning. Hubert said, "I'll take you." Thus began our most interesting introduction to Eastern Tennessee, its ancient feuds, Little and Big Bald; the way of life in Erwin, as told by the cafeteria waitress; the reason for the name Devil Fork Gap; and the various attractions that would draw us again to Eastern Tennessee.

Hubert Metcalf, a slender six-footer, was a shipping clerk for a small manufacturer in the Sams Gap area. However, he had not worked since April, a full three months off with low-back problems. The Veterans Hospital wouldn't give him a release to go back to work, nor would his family doctor. So he was available to drive the transient hiker between gaps. As he said, he meets many of the hikers coming through even though he doesn't live right on the Trail. Apparently, when they get into trouble, they "come off the mountain" looking for help, and Hubert's there.

He told us that the Metcalfs came over on a boat from Ireland, his great grand-daddy being the first, about 100 years ago. The Metcalfs were cooks and some of them are "little-eye" people. This means that some of them have droopy eyelids—sometimes just one. Hubert's grand-daddy, on his mother's side, was an Indian. Hubert, himself, had noticeable traces of Indian blood, dark skin and high cheek bones. He was six feet tall, whereas most Metcalfs were small, fair, and stocky. Hubert married a Rice girl, whose family was also from Ireland and settled in the Sams Gap area, on the North Carolina side. The Rices did not come over on the same boat with the Metcalfs.

On the same boat with the Metcalfs were the Sheltons, who settled in the same area. As Hubert drove us from Sams Gap to Devil Fork, he told us the story behind the name of the community. He said, "You know, you may get home and wonder why some of these places are called what they are. There's been a man killed for every curve in this road and it's as crooked as a black snake."

When we arrived at Devil Fork and located the entrance point of the Appalachian Trail leading eight miles across country to Sams Gap, we noticed that the Trail coursed between two parallel lines of fences, only six feet apart. I asked Hubert why this should be. He said that probably there was a dispute between the neighbors over where the property line was; or it could be that when one neighbor decided to build his fence, the other neighbor refused to help or pay one-half. Consequently, the first neighbor would not let the other share the fence. So, the second neighbor had to build his own, to avoid a hassle. The result is that there is a six-foot lane between two fences, marching up the hill into the woods, and the Appalachian Trail has its fanciest and most luxurious section going south from Devil Fork!

On our ride with Hubert from Sams Gap to Spivey Gap, he told us of his hiking trips in the Big Bald country. He, like most of the people of eastern Tennessee, has a very great respect for the mountains. "They're dangerous—they'll kill you." He warned us that there are two kinds of snakes to be wary of, the copperhead and the rattlesnake. "Now, the copperhead won't warn you afore he bites you. But he won't go out of his way to attack you. But if you step on him or near him, he'll bite you on the foot or leg. You'd be smart if you had some kind of remedy along with you."

One day he was taking his kids for a hike in the mountains. One of his little boys pushed out ahead and was about to step into some bushes. Hubert reached out and grabbed him and hauled him back, just as he was about to step on a copperhead. Hubert figured he had saved the boy's life or at least from being deathly sick from a snake bite. But he was terribly frustrated that he didn't have a gun with him and couldn't find a rock or stick to kill the snake.

As for rattlesnakes, "Before they bite, they'll always warn you with a rattling kind of noise." Hubert has his own special kind of treatment for snake bites, one he learned from his daddy. He

Why did they build two fences along this part of the Trail?

carries salt and turpentine in his pick-up all the time.

The story that had been handed down from father to son was this: A man was on the mountain one day and he stopped to get a drink of water from a spring. He lay down by the spring, and as he was drinking, a rattlesnake bit him on the side of his head. He felt he was going to die. He got deathly sick and finally laid his head on a bag of salt which he happened to have with him. He fell asleep, with the snake bite place right on the salt and "when he woke up he wasn't hardly sick any more and walked off the mountain. That salt drawed all the poison right out of his head!" Ever since, Hubert relies on salt and he adds turpentine "because it draws good too." Neither Hubert nor anybody else in his own family has ever been bitten by a snake.

While we were searching for our entry point of the Appalachian Trail at Spivey Gap, Hubert told us of his hiking in the Army. He entered as an infantryman. Later he became a member of the Motorized Infantry. One of the training missions the infantrymen had to go through was the "forced march." This was a thirty-mile march at a fast pace, with a ten-minute rest every hour. Ambulances trailed the platoon to pick up the ones who faltered and couldn't finish. After a few hours of this particular forced march, Hubert was one of only six or seven who were still going. The leader was a Colonel, also from North Carolina. The Colonel, after about the sixth rest period, turned to Hubert and said, "Looks like only us hillbillies are gonna finish this march!" Hubert said that he will remember what the Colonel said all his life.

One of the reasons that the people around Sams Gap go up the trails on the mountains is to find the "Ginseng Weed." This is a rare plant that is believed to have some medical value. Hubert's family still go looking for the plant and have even transplanted some along their fences.

Our guide book warned us to avoid coming off Big Bald by way of the northwest spur. There's a story about Grier's Rock on that spur, about a man who hid out there for years. Grier's Rock was named after an Indian called John Grier; naturally, he was known as "Injun John." Probably the area is still used as a hide-out.

Hubert classifies himself as a "Music-Maker"; he plays the guitar and the banjo. Apparently in the old days one of the favorite pastimes of the Metcalfs and the Hensleys and the Sheltons was music-making.

After making arrangements to meet Hubert the next morning, we drove on to Erwin, Tennessee, about a half-hour from Sams Gap. We found the inn we were looking for but it had been turned into a bank the prior year. So we settled for a motel, which was well-situated in town, just one block from a cafeteria-restaurant.

Before going to dinner we drove around town to get a feel of it. We guessed it had a population of 10,000; it looked prosperous, clean, and well-disciplined. We saw no slums in the town. We did notice that the YMCA was in the middle of its annual fund raising campaign, with banners flying high. The emphasis was on youth but adults seemed heavily involved in the campaign and in the use of the facilities. The teenagers on the street were in frazzled dungaree shorts, boys shirtless and shoeless; but no long hair or beards.

In practically every driveway there were two cars, one a sedan, the other a pick-up truck. The men all seemed to drive the pick-ups.

Erwin is a town of distinction; it is probably the only town in the western hemisphere that has tried, found guilty, and hanged an elephant. Some years ago a circus was in town. One of the animal acts involved an elephant and his trainer. The elephant went berserk one day and killed his trainer. The local town fathers, to assure that justice prevailed, saw no recourse other than to use the established legal procedures. So the elephant was brought to trial, found guilty of murder, and duly hanged on a railroad derrick in public on the appointed day. (Another version places the killing and the trial in Kingsport, a neighboring town, with the condemned transferred to Erwin for execution on the nearest derrick gallows.)

...They hanged the killer elephant on a derrick like this.

The morning came for our first day's hike from Spivey Gap
across to Sams Gap, a published distance of eleven and one-half
miles across the tops of Little Bald and Big Bald. Hubert advised
us not to leave our car parked alongside the road at Sams Gap. He
said this is a community of good people, but last year somebody
left his car parked there and when he got back he found that the
car had been stripped by a thief. So we parked our car in front of
Hubert's cousin's house, just a stone's throw below the gap. This
was done with the cousin's permission and his assurance that he
would keep an eye on it.

We transferred to Hubert's brand new one-ton pick-up truck
and he drove us the twenty-odd miles around to Spivey Gap where
we started the hike at nine-fifteen a.m.

The Big Bald is worth climbing. As its name suggests, no trees grow on its top. However, it is rich with black soil and matted cover growth. From the summit the view of the peaks and ranges of the Pisgah and the Great Smokies is great. To get to the summit takes about four hours of steady climb from Spivey Gap across the top of Little Bald.

The Trail crosses no streams in this segment because it traverses the eastern watershed divide, which is also the state line separating Tennessee from North Carolina. A wire fence runs along this line separating the two states through most of this segment. The properties on both sides are privately owned. Except when crossing the Big Bald, the Trail runs through broadleafed forests, with scatterings of spruce and pine. We were grateful for the shaded woods for this July hike.

Our second day of hiking this part of the Appalachian Trail was from Devil Fork north to Sams Gap, about eight miles. This was up and down, up and down, for six hours. The only extended steep ascent was for about one hour at the beginning of the day. Again, the Trail generally followed the Tennessee-North Carolina state line, with a fence separating the two. However, the Trail did cut through a couple of farms, owned by Sheltons, and it was obvious that farmers from both states let their cows graze in the fields and woods adjoining the Trail. In addition to crossing the state-line fence, we frequently had to climb through, over or under property-line barbed wire fences, with no convenient gates.

At the end of the hike we came upon the cemetery at Sams Gap. The headstones of the Metcalfs and the Hensleys predominated. In many cases, the Metcalf men's military service and rank were recorded even though their deaths were of natural causes and had occurred many years after completing military service. It seems that military service continues to be an honorable career in the land of the Metcalfs and the Hensleys and, of course, in eastern Tennessee, the land of Sergeant York.

Off we go—green as the wild green yonder

L ittle did we know as we set off on our first hike on the Trail that we wouldn't come even close to making a dinner date that night. It was late November, the days were getting shorter, and we had to hike the last hour in pitch-black darkness. Tah would stand by a tree with the AT white-painted blaze on it until I walked ahead and found the next one. I would then call to her to come ahead.

I had to use my most persuasive powers to keep her moving. At one point we approached a camp site which was occupied by a troop of Boy Scouts. Tah announced that she was going to ask them to take us in for the night. It would count as their good deed for the day, she figured. I talked her out of it and we continued feeling our way from one two-inch by six-inch white-painted marker to the next.

We had arisen leisurely that Sunday morning, in the late fall, with no definite plan in mind for the day. At breakfast we decided to get out of New York City, drive out into the country and maybe do some hiking. We remembered that only a month earlier at Bromley, Vermont we had hiked a couple of hours out and back on the Appalachian Trail during foliage season; and we had half-jokingly talked of hiking the whole 2,100 miles. "So, let's hike a segment of the Trail today," we said. We promptly started driving to Bear Mountain Bridge, an hour away.

We selected a place to hike and drove to the intersection of the AT and Route 9 east of Bear Mountain Bridge in Graymoor, N.Y. By then it was eleven o'clock. Fortunately, we found Mrs. Marcinak. We had stopped at her house because it appeared that the place was a repair shop and we hoped that the owner might be willing to shuttle us for a fee or at least recommend someone to do it. Her husband was busy but she seemed glad to drop the house chores. She followed us as we drove our car to a restaurant nearby where the Trail crossed the highway. We parked there, locked our car and she then drove us in her car to our entry point at Fahnestock State Park. Along the way she told us about the Graymoor Monastery, where she used to work and where through-hikers were welcomed to spend the night.

Mrs. Marcinak did not want to be paid, but we insisted on her taking enough money to replenish her gasoline tank.

We probably did not realize it then, but this first shuttle experience set a pattern we were to follow time and time again in the future. This technique of parking our car at our intended exit point, and then riding with someone else in his or her car to the starting point, permitted us to hike in confidence to the end of the

30

How to have a car waiting at the end of a day's hike—find someone locally, like Mrs. Marcinak of Graymoor, above, who will follow you to the intended exit point where you will park and lock your car. The local person then shuttles you to the entry point of the hike.

day knowing for sure that we had transportation waiting for us. Subsequently, we tried it the other way, parking our car at a starting point, and found it a big waste of time trying to hitch a ride back to our car from the exit point.

This first "formal" hike on the Appalachian Trail was nearly a disaster. It was such an excruciatingly poor experience that it's a wonder that we ever tried it again.

The first major blooper was my failure to plan properly. I tried to make a hiking plan based solely on a road map which does not give simple essentials like trail mileage, topography or landmarks. I estimated the trail mileage to be nine and one-half miles with minor variations in elevation. At an average of three miles per hour, the hike figured to be about three hours. Therefore, if we started at eleven-thirty a.m., we should finish well before dark and in time to drive home, change clothes and then meet Tah's parents at The Brooklyn Club for dinner at seven-thirty p.m. A neat and tidy plan.

But the estimated distance was wrong. The Trail appeared on the road map to be the hypotenuse of a right triangle, with (a) Route 9, about eight miles, and (b) Route 301, about five miles. So, $a^2 + b^2 = c^2$; therefore, c^2 is 89 and c or the hypotenuse is about nine and one-half miles. The main fault with this is that the AT does not go in a straight line along the hypotenuse! It wanders around several extra miles in this case. And I underestimated (a) and (b). Our Trail distance was closer to fourteen miles. My estimate was nearly 50 percent wrong.

My second major miscalculation was to plan on hiking three miles an hour. That might do for relatively flat terrain and for short distances. But the terrain between Fahnestock and Graymoor, even though not terribly rugged, is not flat by any stretch of the imagination. And without a light you do have to slow down considerably after dark! My estimate of our rate of walking was overstated at least 50 percent.

I began to realize that we had a problem when we ran into an architect at a junction of the Trail and a county road. I asked him how far it was to Route 9 and he guessed five to six miles. I said, "How can that be when we just passed Indian Lake back there, which should leave only a couple of miles at most?" He said, "I'm sorry to tell you that Indian Lake is still ahead of you. The lake to your rear is Oscawana Lake." What a blow!

We finally emerged at our parked car at six-thirty p.m. The best we could do was call The Brooklyn Club and leave a message for Sonni and Ernst Weber, Tah's parents, apologizing for our failure to show. Tah still remembers the hike vividly and reminds me that I was 50 percent wrong on distance and 50 percent wrong on speed. Therefore, she says that I was 100 percent wrong altogether!

The next fall, on our annual pilgrimage to New England during foliage season, we took along ATC's New Hampshire-Vermont Guide. It helped us become more deeply involved in getting started on the Trail.

We ate our cake and had it, too

We *could* have slept every night in a shelter like the one below—but didn't, as you can see at the left. Our initial philosophy had been that at the end of every hike we would return to a nice warm-in-winter or cool-in-summer room, warm bath, cocktails with ice before a hot dinner served at a table, and to a soft bed. We are great for the outdoors during daylight hours, but come nightfall, we're definitely unfurred animals, we said.

Alas, in hiking, as in real life, one is faced with choices requiring decisions. Our first few days on the Trail made this clear: Unwillingness to backpack was causing us certain inconveniences and wasted efforts during hiking days. We had to choose between camping out on the Trail occasionally and hiking many extra miles off the Trail solely to get to the amenities of a motel room, including cocktails with ice.

We had listened with envy to our son, Jim, tell of his backpack trip into the Canadian Rockies a few years earlier. He had taken a six-week trip alone during the summer after finishing graduate school in 1968. In a way, it was an extension of a camping trip with the rest of the family through the west and northwest some six years earlier. But this time he had set out alone to the wilderness to "find himself," and he did. As he put it, "I came to know myself, my strengths and weaknesses, as I had never known before."

At the end of those six weeks, he joined Tah, Suzanne and me in Seattle, Washington, whence we set out on a horse-backpack trip through the wilderness of the North Cascades. He was so uncomfortable (and I believe embarrassed) riding a horse, with a couple of pack horses trailing, that frequently he dismounted and led his horse. He considered riding to be "cheating."

Our memory of his enthusiasm for backpacking had been haunting. Is it only for the young? Why should not the parents enjoy the pleasures of the children?

Soon after Jim and Betsy married, they began hiking the high country of the Sierras. Their letters and tapes rang out the "joy of walking versus the pleasure of riding." We had walked with them for a few days the previous spring and had sat in the meadow atop a hill and reveled in the sounds of non-mechanical, natural things. It was infectious.

Then, of course, Jim and Betsy nudged us closer by the birthday gift of "The Complete Walker" by Colin Fletcher.* Somehow or other, the elated description by Fletcher of a house on one's back was fetching. We read the book and sorted out in our minds what our styles of architecture, furnishing and decorating would be...*if* we changed our minds and became backpackers. We were

*Published by Alfred A. Knopf, Inc., 1968

also faced with the fact that three major segments of the Appalachian Trail had to be backpacked: the Smokies, sections of the White Mountains where no huts were open, and long stretches in Maine.

Tah's earliest recollection of backpacking is of the time when her parents arranged for two Austrian peasants to backpack her and her sister, Greta, at ages eight and six, up the mountain from Oetz to Piburg in Austria. Tah rode backwards, on the back of the packer, up the steep inclines and over the monstrous boulders of the area. Not until they reached Piburg did she know that the reason for the trip was that the two girls were suspected of having diptheria. It was a dread disease; the very mention of it would have caused panic in the village. So, the family had decided that the best thing was to take the girls up the mountain where, first, there would be the expert diagnosis and treatment capability available—Uncle Meinhard at Piburg was a pediatrician—and second, at Piburg they would be in isolation and present no epidemic threat to the villagers. As it turned out, no diptheria, but a subconscious anti-backpacking syndrome may have been planted in Tah.

Yet, in Tah's case, a stronger syndrome for high places and the quietude (or noises) of natural settings prevailed. A certain degree of light-headedness or cut-free spirit develops in her as she gains altitude. It's kind of like a "trip." So when it comes down to a choice of giving up end-of-day comforts, on the one hand, in order to have more wilderness experiences at high altitudes, on the other, Tah's leanings are strongly towards the latter.

In my own case, I grew up roughing it. Weekend camping trips were frequent and enjoyable, but usually for the purpose of hunting or fishing and not for walking as the pleasure event. One of the most valuable gifts my father gave me was the experience of living the way of the wilderness. From my youngest days, Pop took me with him, adventuring into the woods—sometimes fishing for sheer fun, but mostly to catch food, and sometimes to hunt wild turkey, a strange sport. One goes deeply into the woods, picks a likely spot, sits, leaning against a tall virgin pine tree, and, on a handmade mouth-organ, pipes out the mating call of the wild turkey. Pretty soon a fat turkey responds and comes galumphing through the trees for a rendezvous of love. Unfairly, I must admit, the turkey is shot and becomes food for a family of six for the next few days.

The hunting and fishing didn't take with me. But the long walks into the woods, the love of the unspoiled wilderness did take. So I leaned strongly, also, towards more wilderness experience even if it meant giving up some end-of-day comforts.

We entered the Skimeister Sport Shop in North Woodstock, N.H., weary from two days of hiking between Kinsman and Franconia Notches, over Wolf, North Kinsman and South Kinsman mountains. To cover this fifteen miles of rugged Appalachian Trail, we had to use two days. Without backpacks we had to hike off the Trail at the end of each day to our car, two extra miles on a sloggy, boggy, log road. What a terribly inefficient way to cover fifteen miles of the Appalachian Trail—three extra hours, wasted hours, to avoid one overnight at a shelter! I'd say that the decision to get equipped to spend an occasional night out was 98 percent made as we entered the shop; nonetheless, we kept the option open until we had seen the equipment.

Adults: People old enough to buy their own toys

With memories of recent discomforts, we entered the Skimeister Sport Shop, still not decided but willing to play "what if" with the shop clerk, reserving decision as long as possible.

We began shopping in the organized way, suggested by Colin Fletcher, to cover the three absolute essentials: 1) the frame and pack (the house on the back), 2) the sleeping gear (the bedroom), and 3) the critical utensils for eating and drinking (the kitchen and pantry). Overriding these essentials was the need for protection against the elements, within reasonable weight limits.

We asked the shop clerk to take us through the options on frames and packs first. The choice was easy on this first essential; we chose the Kelty, medium for Tah and large for me. Our packs have five outside pockets, two small ones on each side and one large one in the back. As Fletcher's book said, we would systematically use each of these outside pockets for certain items, such as one pocket for medical and snake bite kits, another for maps and trail guides, and the others for often-needed items which could be easily reached without unpacking the main compartment.

We turned to the second essential, the sleeping gear. The choice of materials was clearer than the shape and construction of the sleeping bags. Both of us tried on several bags, right in the middle of the salesroom. The down-filled, nylon-covered bag was

41

it. Tah immediately chose the mummy style, because of the hood, and because she readily saw that if she wanted to turn, the bag would turn with her. I wanted room to turn at will inside the bag. I chose the more standard shape, with no hood.

It occurred to me that someday, somebody will split the lower end of the mummy bag and sew the two parts into two legs; result, the hiker would put on his sleeping bag to go to bed. Subsequently, I have been told that this is not a good idea because conservation of heat is more efficiently maintained by having a single compartment for the entire body.

We spent little shopping time on the third essential, eating and drinking equipment, as we already had some trail experience with lunches and water bottles. As it turned out, we should have spent more shopping time on this essential.

We bit the bullet, decided to go backpacking, paid our money and walked out of the Skimeister committed, hooked and anxious to try it out. We started the next day.

For our first backpack trip we chose Mt. Moosilauke, the real feature mountain between the Presidential Range of the White Mountains to the north in New Hampshire and the Green Mountains of Vermont to the southwest. Every member of the Dartmouth Outing Club (DOC) throughout the ages has taken Moosilauke in as a part of his life. Freshman members are assigned to trail-crews, and the trails up and down this mountain are undoubtedly among the best marked and best manicured in the east. The Appalachian Trail incorporated the DOC trail into its own system and the markings are dual, with the orange and black of DOC and the white paint slash of the Appalachian Trail.

Our plan was that we would climb Moosilauke, and spend the night at the DOC cabin, nearly seven miles from our entry point of Kinsman Notch. The second day we would arise early and continue to the foot of Mt. Cube, a distance of fourteen miles of easy terrain.

After our shopping spree in the Skimeister, we returned to our headquarters in the Franconia Notch area, The Horse and Hound Inn. Upon arrival earlier in the week, I had discussed with Ira Stroup, the owner, the prospects of our staying there, explaining that Tah and I were hiking the Appalachian Trail and needed transportation each day to the entry point. When he said he'd

We bought the toys—Could we make them work?

The Horse and Hound Inn, in the tradition of small New England inns, was delightful even after the foliage season had come and gone. This was our home in Franconia Notch, N.H. while we were learning to backpack.

drive us, we had a deal, regardless of any other conditions or services offered. It was a good choice. We stayed the full week.

Ira and his wife had come to The Horse and Hound nineteen years earlier and their two children had been born in Franconia. The Inn had just finished a strong fall season with Foliage Weekend on Columbus Day. The help had been cut to a skeleton crew as fewer than six rooms were expected to be occupied.

The post-season routine was to clean the rooms every other day. As we checked in, we found our nice corner room only partially ready, no towels, no soap and few clothes hangers. Tah and I foraged for ourselves, stripping the empty room next door of needed items to complete ours.

Dinner on our second night at the Inn could have almost been classified as "catastrophic." Relatively few guests were staying overnight. However, because the Inn has a reputation for fine food, guests enough to fill eighteen tables had turned up unexpectedly at seven p.m., with only two waitresses and a slow cook aboard. Furthermore, the piano player had quit. But this deficiency was happily covered by a lady guest filling in to the applause of the waiting diners.

There was a two-hour wait for people who arrived at seven-thirty or later, including three people from Chicago, a newlywed couple who obviously preferred to eat early, and us. Beverly, a therapist by trade, was filling in time before her planned marriage to a bartender in November. She was acting as assistant V.P. or Maitre d' and rushing around and through the dining room consoling guests and cajoling the cook and the waitresses. Later, we found that she was also the chamber-maid and room-service bellhop. Despite the long wait, the food was excellent. But, we vowed to be in the dining room first from then on.

At Tah's suggestion, the night before our first backpack trip, we drove our car to our planned southern exit point, on Route 25A at the northern foot of Mt. Cube. It took forty-five miles of driving one way in two cars to park our car at the exit point of a twenty-one mile hike. We returned in Ira's car which he had loaned us. That night we dreamed uneasy dreams of the rigors of Moosilauke—the book used language which we respect, e.g., "rough terrrain," "rough underfoot," "be careful climbing the ladders," and "dangerous in winter," all harsh language.

We got to the entrance of the Trail at eight-fifteen a.m., Saturday. The book had overstated the conditions. The author of this section was more dramatic than other authors using the same adjectives for other segments of the Trail. Yes, there were a few short ladders to climb, but the DOC had thoughtfully added a steel cable alongside for hand-holding.

I had remembered to pull up the hip straps of my backpack so tightly that they hurt. This, of course, was to get the bulk of the weight load onto the hips and off the shoulders. After about a half-hour Tah complained that her pack was constantly banging the back of her head and that she was feeling like a yoked ox. We stopped long enough to lower her pack frame about six inches, off her waist down to her hips, and to tighten the shoulder straps. This created a whole new outlook for her. She could now hold her head up normally and the pack stopped swaying from side to side with each step. She no longer was a yoked ox.

One of the early things we had to learn was that with a new center of gravity and with the inertia of the pack, our feet were repeatedly landing at unexpected points. This became important in stepping from high stones to low stones in boggy terrain!

It's a steep, steady climb up Moosilauke. During the first three hours, at least forty youths passed and repassed us on the way. One group was a scout troop from Chelmsford, Massachusetts. We re-enacted the story of the Tortoise and the Hare. By the time we got to the top, over one hundred people had collected in their own separate groups, having lunch. One scout group was pitching tents for the night near the DOC winter cabin.

We took a leisurely lunch break. The view in all directions was spectacular and the temperature was between 55° and 60°, in bright sunshine. *And we were tired,* shoulders, hips, calves, and ankles, but we had only three and one-half miles to go, and all downhill. So when we took off at two p.m. we anticipated at most a two-hour descent to a campsite at another DOC cabin.

The descent was sharp, rugged and slow. Instead of a two-hour descent, we took three hours and the last hour tested our endurance mightily. Finally, after two hours and fifty-five minutes, I was sorely leaning towards pitching a camp on the Trail, fully believing that we might have missed the turn-off to the cabin. But at that moment, Tah said, "Listen! I heard the sound of chopping wood! The cabin must be close ahead!'' We persevered and five minutes later, there it was! A young Dartmouth junior named Dave from Kenosha, Wisconsin was, indeed, chopping firewood while his girl friend, Doreen, was starting a fire for the evening meal in front of the cabin. What a welcome sight!

We pitched camp by a clear stream, just a hundred yards below the DOC cabin. On the whole, our first night out went well. But we did learn several things. The pre-packaged dinner of dehydrated foods could have served four people. It contained an orange drink, soup, stew with dumplings, and butterscotch pudding. We could have used a third pot or sauce pan. For coffee and for soup we should have had hard plastic cups instead of the folding water cups, which leaked. We had brought a plastic water flask, but we needed an extra one, since we had filled the one with booze, which we had to drink before filling the flask with water. After that, whatever problems we had seemed to diminish in importance. Afterwards, we decided that we should make up a checklist for packing, as we had left behind all eating utensils. We also decided not to carry six oranges and six apples on future trips. Nor would we have more than one change of clothing for up to a week's trip.

The second day started at nine a.m. and ended fourteen miles and eight hours later. We then vowed that six hours a day of strenuous hiking, regardless of the miles, was about all we wanted to do. We solemnly promised ourselves to stop in mid-afternoon rather than at five p.m. This was not a realistic promise! As usual we broke such vows and promises.

At the end of our first backpacking adventure we headed toward Southern New England, as it was well past the middle of October and the fall colors were flowing south. We were smugly content that grandparents like us could learn new tricks.

Mahoosuc Notch:
the toughest mile

Even without the snow, this was an obstacle course that could separate the men from the boys—but not, in our case, the men from the women. We licked this character-tester with teamwork, as you can judge from Tah's letter to the family.

Dear Family:

Remember I told you that last year in October we had been chased out of Maine by the cold weather! Well, we went back a little earlier this year and took up where we left off, at Grafton Notch, heading south over Old Speck Mountain and through Mahoosuc Notch.

First day of our five-day backpack trip (up Old Speck Mountain): Going up was nice but going down was extremely steep and rough, and endless. The Maine miles are twice as long as anywhere else. I am getting psyched out about going through the Mahoosuc Notch tomorrow. For hundreds of miles the reputation of the Notch is terrible; tales of horror; going through tunnels, climbing up and down huge boulders, etc.

Second day—The Mahoosuc Notch (Speck Pond Shelter through the Notch to Full Goose Shelter): My fears are well-founded; it was worse than expected! The Notch is only one mile long and it took us three hours!! First of all, before the Notch, there was an hour's steep descent to the Notch; and then, I couldn't believe it, endless boulders, the size of outhouses, all tumbled about. We had to go over and under them, into caves and tunnels so small and narrow

What kept us going: the vision of a hot fire and a cold drink.

we had to take off our packs and push them through ahead of us. It was all rock-climbing and gymnastics, chinning ourselves with fully loaded backpacks up perpendicular rocks of ten feet and then lowering ourselves with pack, perpendicularly, naturally, down about eight feet; continue level for a bit before ascending another nine-foot boulder, with perhaps eighteen inches level before descending ten feet, perpendicular, naturally, and then through a cave, etc., etc. This went on endlessly. We stopped amid this mess to rest and eat something. After two hours I was obviously slowing down; my muscles were aching. I thought I just could not haul myself and pack up another one of those huge boulders. Jim would go ahead and help me by lifting and tugging me by my backpack. Finally, it became obvious I could not continue with the pack. So poor Jim, while having his pack on his back, would hurl my pack up ten feet; climb up after it; wait for me; then hurl my pack down the next cave, take off his and push his through; then crawl through himself. I repeat; it was an experience! Three hours! After we got through the Notch, I put on my pack again and then we were faced with the product of a "diabolic mind." The person who laid out the Trail out of the Notch laid the Trail straight up, but straight up. We "scratched and clawed" our way up the mountain. We had left Speck Pond Shelter at eight a.m. and arrived at Full Goose Shelter at four p.m....we were so relieved to get there. Most people go through the Notch in two hours, or less. We had to rest more than the twenty-year-old kids. If Jim had not taken my backpack the last one-third of the way, I still would be there. What is so maddening is that the whole day's hike covered only five miles!!! Horizontal miles, that is! It must have been one million miles counting all the footage, up and down.

Everybody gets psyched out on the difficulties of the Mahoosuc Notch and Old Speck Mountain. Now that we have done it, we can wax philosophical about it. The Notch's tough reputation is fully deserved in many respects, but its beauty is seldomly praised. It's natural to talk only about how hard it is to go through, over, under and around enormous boulders. The Notch is a grand expression of nature, a partial collapsing of the sheer walls of mountains on each side of a canyon. It has character and tends to build character in hikers.

Love,

KEF

Enough
wasn't enough

When we left Monson General Store in Monson, Maine, we thought we had food to burn. Later, how we wished we had bought more...

Prospects of running out of food and being unable to travel because of a sprained ankle, while still thirty-five miles deep in the wilderness of Maine, start some serious thinking. Our thoughts were about the basic proposition of the survival of the fittest, ethics of survival, predators, the role of tools in man's survival, and the role of tools in the animal world.

We were beyond the point of no return on a 100-mile hike, from Monson to Abol Bridge, Maine. Ten days of provisions had already been stretched to twelve days; now they must be stretched some more if Tah's sprained ankle prevented travel for a few days. We were faced with the decision of dividing up what little food was left and my hiking thirty-five miles to get help while Tah holed up

With food running low...

immobile in a deserted fishing cabin.

That night before we went to bed, we prepared for my leaving at daybreak to go for help. We divided the food. I gathered firewood for the stove and filled containers with fresh water from the lake. Tah had sprained her ankle in a bog seven miles south of The Antlers, an abandoned sporting camp on Lower Jo-Mary Lake. Fortunately she had been able to limp all the way into camp before her ankle got so sore that she could not put any weight on it. The cabin was in surprisingly good shape, even though windows were broken and doors were missing. The roof appeared water-proof and there were two cot-beds with mattresses. Most impor-tantly there was plenty of fresh water at hand. It was an ideal shelter to sweat out a crisis such as we faced.

At daybreak the next morning, Tah arose with me and tested her ankle. She found that she could put some of her weight on it! We agreed that we would invest one more day in rest at the cabin before I took off for help. She guessed that there was a 60% chance that she could hike out of the wilderness. This was unques-tionably the most desirable alternative. It was during this day of rest that the serious thoughts about survival began to flow.

I was confident of our alternatives; we could hike out together; or send a message to a ranger by one of the through-hikers, or I could hike out to rent a charter float-plane to come back to pick up Tah. Clearly we could resolve the situation in three to four days, at the end of which we might be a bit hungry but really no worse for wear. We reminded ourselves that Mahatma Gandhi fasted for two or three months. As long as we had water, there was no real physiological danger.

However, it was not an absolute certainty that we would resolve the situation in three or four days. It might be wise to assume that it would take longer. If so, what should we be doing? The only pressing problem we faced was a shortage of food. Wood for fires was in ample supply and nearby. Wintry weather was still at least thirty days away.

There were obvious potential sources for food: fish from the lake, small animals and birds from the woods. We found ourselves woefully uninformed on edible roots and plants. However, we knew that fish and game were plentiful if we could devise ways of catching or trapping them.

The easiest food source was fish from the lake, using fishhooks and worms or insects. Surely there must be fishhooks around an abandoned fishing camp! An hour's searching of the area—of the fallen and the upright walls and the shelves of the cabins, even of the alder bushes for possible back-lashes—was to no avail. There were no fishhooks anywhere. What about making a fishhook out of a safety-pin? This was a possibility, but it was a last resort idea because a hook really needs a barb on it to prevent the fish from "throwing" the hook. A safety-pin hook backed up by a dip net might do to catch fish in shallow water. We really should have had an emergency kit in our backpacks. Such a kit would have contained fishhooks and lines.

From the discarded rubbish lying around, I rigged a fish trap, using an old metal milk crate and wrapping it with screen wire from a cabin window. Into it I fashioned a tapered funnel. Fish will swim into the larger end of a funnel to bait and then can not maneuver their way out again. I baited the trap with a few precious raisins and placed it in three feet of water in the lake. After about an hour, lo and behold, a small fish swam into the trap. It was too small to add much protein to our diet, but it was ideal for bait, not only for the fish trap, but also for the animal trap which I was making.

Later I checked the fish-baited trap and found it not only empty but also battered by the waves. The funnel had become completely separated. So I pulled the trap and abandoned the project. Even so, it was clear to me that if it became necessary I could devise a trap to catch enough fish to assure survival!

During the day I worked on an animal trap, conjuring up the design of a home-made trap which my father built. It had a trip mechanism, set off or tripped by the animal's gnawing on a piece of meat attached to the trigger. This caused the box-trap to fall over the animal, trapping him inside. By using a wooden bushel basket, two notched sticks, a leather thong shoe-string and a piece of fish as bait, I rigged a trap which might have worked. We never gave it a chance because we decided definitely to start hiking out the next morning.

While working on these traps, I searched my memory for animals which use tools and traps to provide food for survival. Seagulls and other birds in marshes and near the sea can be said to

...I started to think of traps.

use tools in opening shell fish. They drop clams or mussels onto stones to open them. The only animal I could think of which uses a trap to catch food is the spider. He spins his web and can leave it for other activities and catch his meals while being occupied elsewhere.

The carnivorous animals survive by being predators, hunting and killing and eating the weaker animals in their habitat. However repulsive to us the kill appears to be, the cold fact is that the lion or wild dog or leopard or cheetah or crocodile must eat to survive and he has no tools or traps. He has limited intelligence and no way to store food except in his stomach or in fat. Therefore, he must kill when hungry. Some of these predator animals stake out territories which they fight for and protect. They have "exclusive" hunting rights there. Others follow herds as they move to and from grazing areas.

We human beings are inclined to have warmer feelings towards herbivorous animals which seem less aggressive and less bloodthirsty. They keep on the move for plants and water and they are subject to being the prey of carnivorous animals. Human beings relish their tender meat. Therefore, herbivorous animals are vulnerable to both carnivorous animals and human beings. They are also more vulnerable to the ravages of drought and forest fires.

Animals without tools or traps or protective equipment are hard put to survive as a species. Their role is made especially difficult with man as their enemy as well as the animals of the forest.

Just imagine earliest and primitive man before he had tools and before he had a developed intelligence. His survival was just as precarious as any other animal's. Without tools and without means of storing food, the overwhelming occupation was hunting for food. No wonder that the proof of manhood was a demonstration of hunting and warrior skills, the latter to protect his hunting territory. There were no other things of such importance to survival.

Of incidental interest while we awaited Tah's improvement was the beginning of changes in my attitude towards friendly animals around the camp. I began to measure the chipmunks, red squirrels and little birds in terms of their nutritional value if needed. I began to take on the attitude of a predator, a carnivorous animal, wondering whether I could develop the confident attack for a successful kill without weapons as other predators do. I did not have to face that test.

Tah was able to walk out of the wilderness, the full thirty-five miles to Abol Bridge. Later, x-rays revealed that her ankle had been broken—a hairline fracture.

Tah had managed beautifully stretching our food from the original ten days to fourteen days. By the twelfth and thirteenth days our meals had become pretty skinny. Breakfast for both of us was one portion of oatmeal plus some dried fruit and one portion of hot chocolate. Lunch consisted of three saltine squares and twelve raisins. Dinner was one-half can of dried beef (four ounces) one package of dried cheese sauce and a bit of rice for both of us. But we made it all the way under our own power.

The Trail is like a song—
　　A ballad, soft and tender and melodic;
　　Of forests and rocks, fields and plains;
　　Of spring rains, summer warmth and fall foliage.
　　Of people on farms; in post offices in cities and towns,
　　On the open roads and wooded trails—
　　Reaching out in friendship, with warm welcomes.
　　Of animals, curious but cautious,
　　Cheerful, industrious and companionable escorts.

The Trail is a robust song—
　　With sometime dissonant notes,
　　Of scrambling ahead of a storm to a shelter;
　　Of slogging through bogs and dodging blowdowns;
　　Of past struggles and defeats,
　　Of hurt and sorrow and disappointments.
　　Of growing pains and rumbles of confrontations;
　　Of scratching and clawing up mountains
　　In search of answers that surely are.

The Trail is a majestic song—
　　Of discoveries of self in the natural world;
　　It soars and carries the hiker to heights,
　　　of indescribable joy,
　　Of being a part of the song,
　　Of helping to create it, produce it and sing it.
　　A majestic song of the promise of ultimate victory.

The Trail is like a song—

A ballad, soft and tender and melodic

We stepped into another world

Most people start hiking the Appalachian Trail in early spring-time at Springer Mountain, Georgia, the southern terminus of the Blue Ridge Mountains and of the Trail. Springer is a well-eroded 3,782-foot slope with no clearly defined peak. Stubby oak trees are scattered about this wilderness area. All of the Trail's eighty miles in Georgia wind in and about the Chattahoochee National Forest across the northern part of the state.

The basic design and maintenance of the sections compare favorably with the best along the entire Trail. The quality is on a level with the sections of the Appalachian Mountain Club in New England, the Dartmouth Outing Club in Vermont and New Hampshire, and the Potomac Appalachian Trail Club in the Shenandoah National Park in Virginia.

In Georgia the spring wild flowers are something to see and

walk among. We saw acre-size fields of trillium, mayapple, bloodroot, bluets, violets and buttercups. We saw one bloodroot flower with twenty-six petals, twenty-six! Fields upon fields of ferns rise out of the forest floor in the shade of newly leafed trees. Around May first, with every 1,000-foot change of elevation along the Trail, the hiker passes from spring to winter and back to spring foliage. Mountain laurel and rhododendron cover large sections of the forest in bloom in late spring and early summer.

Spring birds are in as great profusion as spring wild flowers. Some we failed to identify. But old friends we heard, saw and rejoiced in—woodpeckers, titmice, white-throated sparrows, towhees, juncos, robins, and an occasional wood thrush singing high in a poplar tree.

One of our hikes in Georgia was twelve miles between Montray Road and Dick's Creek Gap. There were very few spring flowers along the way, possibly because of the poor quality of the soil. The feature of this segment is 4,200-foot Montray, the name of which is an interesting example of metamorphosis in language. Its name is gradually becoming Tray Mountain. Even the geodetic marker at the peak lists Tray Mountain. It seems clear that it originally was designated the French name of Mont Ray. An old sign reads Montray Lean-to and the guide book encloses Tray Mountain in parenthesis.

Bavaria? No. Helen, Georgia. One of many wonderful base camps

After a week of day-hiking at one point, we took a day off to do laundry and to rest. Anyway, the weather prediction was for rain and possibly severe thunderstorms. We were staying in a motel in a small town named Helen, which in recent times is being called Alpine Helen. It is a "Gateway to the Chattahoochee National Forest" for travelers coming from central and southern Georgia. Helen was an ordinary, run-of-the-mill southern, small

town until Pete Hodkinson took charge of it and turned it into an Alpine village. He had to get the cooperation of everybody in town plus some bankers and friendly investors out of town, and most importantly, he needed the imagination and artistic skills of one John Kollock. John was a painter and a historian of North Georgia and when he was asked for ideas on improving the looks of the town, he was responsive with an idea he had eighteen years

earlier. He brought forth memories of Bavaria, Germany when he had been stationed there in the Army. Within a week he delivered watercolor sketches of the buildings in the town of Helen in an Alpine style. The merchants and town officials accepted John's ideas readily and Helen became the Alpine village it is today. They adopted signage control and prohibited neon advertising. (The one exception stands out like a sore thumb, the service station in the middle of town, with a string of neon lights along the Alpine roof line!)

Subsequently, Pete Hodkinson built the Helendorf, a super motel-hotel combination in Bavarian style. To finance the venture, he sold each room in advance as a condominium.

Local citizens say that Pete alienated some people, but most praise him for getting things done. Everyone enjoys the huge increase in tourism in Helen.

Unfortunately, Pete is not around any longer to enjoy the successes of Alpine Helen. He had organized an annual "Helen-to-the-Atlantic Ocean" balloon race which became a popular event with entrants from far and wide. Pete himself was an enthusiastic participant, but he had the misfortune of landing his balloon on some high tension wires and was killed in the crash.

To do our laundry we drove a few miles south to Clarkesville. As luck would have it, the automatic laundry was in the same block as the office of Dr. Tom Hodges, the father of Phillip, whom we had met frequently on the Trail. Dr. Tom, even though he had no idea of who we were except that we knew his son, was most gracious and urged us to go to his house for a visit with Phillip and Mrs. Hodges. He would try to round up Phillip and let him know that we were here. We are sure that Dr. and Mrs. Hodges have gone through these "drop-in" friends from the AT dozens of times. Phillip and his three hiking companions had been so friendly that people wanted to see them again. The long and short of our visit to Clarkesville is that we did not see Phillip. He could not be found. He and his girl-friend had left no messages about their whereabouts. After a lovely lunch and visit, we departed and requested Mrs. Hodges to give Phillip our best. She replied, "I'll give him your best and my worst!"*

*Phillip married the girl. About a year later we received an announcement of the marriage of Donna Carol and Philip Stone.

The Southern Appalachian Mountains in the Nantahalas, Great Smokies, Pisgah and Cherokee are among the "most rugged segments of the entire Appalachian chain. Except perhaps for Maine, it represents the superlative in the 'Wilderness' and the primitive made available by the Appalachian Trail....Perhaps apart from the endless ridges (long distances are above 5,000 feet elevation), the most impressive feature of trail travel in the

To return to nature is to intrude

Southern Appalachians is the profusion of flowering shrubs—rhododendron, azalea and laurel.''* To enjoy those flowering shrubs, one has to hike these sections in late spring and early summer.

*Appalachian Trail Conference Guide to the Appalachian Trail in Tennessee and North Carolina, publication No. 24, third edition, pp. 2 and 3.

The thirteen-mile hike between Mooney and Deep Gaps was on graded trails, pleasant hiking. Ferns were beginning to unfurl; bluets were strewn alongside our path. It was a cool but bright spring day. We talked to a dozen or so hikers during the day, but only four planned to go all the way. Two of these were a young bearded man and his female companion who were hiking with two dogs. Since dogs are forbidden in the Great Smoky Mountains National Park, they planned to hitch-hike around the Park. Their plan was to hike until mid-August and then leap-frog to Katahdin, Maine and start walking south. This way they would have a good chance to finish before cold weather drove them off the Trail.

We were reminded of this couple and their two dogs later, when in the Shenandoah National Park, we met a young couple hiking the Trail with their baby and one dog. The mother was carrying the infant (still being breast-fed) in a pack on her back. The father carried all the gear and food required for camping at night. The dog had his own Kelty pack, which was filled with his own food and with diapers for the baby. This foursome had a date the following day at the junction of the Trail and U.S. Route 522 in Chester Gap to be picked up by the mother's sister. The family had not decided whether to hike the entire Trail.

Creatures of the forests consider man an intruder. They don't know how to chase him out of their domain. But they have protective instincts to help their newborn survive when man gets too close. We were delightfully impressed on a day-hike in the Nantahalas by a seductive white-tailed doe and a mama grouse. As we rounded a corner, the doe leapt across the Trail just ahead. She came to a halt thirty yards in front of us and alongside the Trail. She looked over her shoulder at us invitingly. "Come chase me." We watched while standing still and she took off again, but only for a few more yards. She again invited us to follow. We caught on that she was trying to lure us away from the newborn which probably was lying quietly nearby.

On the same hike, we flushed a grouse which no sooner became airborne than she landed again and fluttered her wings loudly. We looked at the spot where she had been when we first saw her, and surely enough there was a tiny, brand new grouselet, playing dead. Mama grouse continued clucking to warn her little one to lie still. We moved on to relieve the tension.

On another day, we came upon a pair of birds with a couple of newly hatched chicks. I could not identify them but they were like the junco. The father bird circled us but mama bird felt that we were entirely too close to her young ones. So she dive-bombed me, coming close to my head, several times, before pulling up.

One day in the Nantahalas, I stopped short of stepping on a copperhead snake, about three feet long and lying along the edge of the Trail. I pondered momentarily what to do about him. I truly felt that he had as much right to be there as I had. And most likely he was serving a more useful purpose in the balancing act of the forest. Without any specific purpose at all, I slipped my walking staff under his belly at mid-point and heaved him thirty feet high into the thick foliage on the downhill side of the Trail. He fell from leafy limb to leafy limb to the ground and scampered away as he landed. I imagined the story he had to tell when he got home that night!

Tom McKay, Supervisor of the Franklin P.O., delivers a "care package" to Tah.

"Care packages": something more to carry, but worth it

The Trail runs mainly on ridges and across mountain peaks of the Appalachian range. But some sections cross fertile valleys, connecting separate ranges of mountains.

The Trail goes right down main street in several small towns, for example: Caratunk, Maine; Monson, Maine; Hanover, N.H.; Duncannon, Pennsylvania; Groseclose, Virginia; Hot Springs, N.C. You get the feeling that the residents of these towns like the routings and want hikers to feel at home in each of them.

Naturally, these towns are key "mail-drops" for through-hikers. Some mail dried foods and clothes to themselves; others get family or friends to mail packages to them on a prearranged schedule.

Franklin, North Carolina is not right on the Trail, but it's within an easy hitch-hike or taxi ride. It is a popular post office stop. Its location is strategic, just over a hundred miles or about a week of hiking from Springer Mountain in Georgia.

The Trail
was full of
surprises

Wesser, N.C. was a surprise to us, in the heart of the Nantahalas, "Land-of-the-Noonday-Sun." We were not at all
prepared for a profusion of whitewater activity, for which Wesser
is a major center. Nantahala Outdoor Center operates a precision
race course laid out in the rapids, rents canoes, kayaks and rafts,
and provides a corps of instructors for all level of skills. The out-
fitters shop is well-stocked for various kinds of outdoor and

wilderness activities. A motel and restaurant cater to hikers as well as water enthusiasts. In season, daily trips are organized for rafters to go to the Chattooga, one of the wildest whitewater rivers and where the movie "Deliverance" was filmed. Off season they arrange group whitewater trips to Central and South America.

The AT in northern Virginia is divided by five gaps: Keys, Snickers, Ashby, Manassas and Chester. These provided convenient entry and exit points for day hikes, even though distances between them varied from six to thirteen miles. Early history centered on the gaps as they afforded passage-ways from the Piedmont in the east to the Shenandoah Valley for Indians, early explorers and railroads, as well as for armies.

One day we hiked south from Manassas Gap to Compton Gap, which is the point where the AT first crosses the Skyline Drive in the northern part of the Shenandoah National Park. At about mid-point of this nine-and-one-half-mile hike, we were completely startled by the posted sign which faced us as we climbed a stile over a fence. The sign warned in part:

Pets on Leash
Stay on Trail
Violators Will Be Eaten

Why this sudden tall fence along the Trail?

To see what's behind it, please turn page...

The Trail skirts even a zoological breeding ground!

I said to Tah, "This must be a joke." But as we proceeded we gained understanding. To our right was a ten-foot high wire fence, behind which were open grazing fields. Our path was through high brush. We felt as though we were in safari-land. The undergrowth was heavy and green. The temperature was steamy. Vines were hanging from trees. Tah said, "I expect howler monkeys to jump out at any moment." Shortly, we saw rolling hills to our right, beyond the tall fence.

We came to a sudden halt! There was a herd of zebras, grazing peacefully! Then we saw camels. "What's going on?" we asked. Aren't we in Virginia? The explanation became clear when we crossed Highway 522. We had hiked through government zoological breeding grounds, operated under the auspices of the Conservation and Research Center of the National Zoological Park.

*Another surprise!
We suddenly
found ourselves...*

Watching the
hawk
watchers

North of Eckville we saw a big bird chasing a little bird, swooping down upon him at intervals with clear intent to destroy the little one. This seemed peculiar. Generally, we had noticed that the little birds chased the big ones away from their territory. But not so in Hawk Mountain Sanctuary! The hawks and eagles are protected during their migratory season and they act every bit like bosses.

Hawks and eagles migrate along the Appalachian Trail on the Kittatinny Ridge in Pennsylvania. To save the birds from slaughter

by "sportsmen" and chicken farmers The Hawk Mountain Association bought 1400 acres on the top of Hawk Mountain near Eckville to establish a sanctuary. Lookout Rock, about two miles off the Trail, is a popular bird-watching spot, especially in late September to early November during the days of heaviest migration. Binoculars are recommended.*

*Condensed from the Second Edition of "Guide to the Appalachian Trail in Pennsylvania," available from the Appalachian Trail Conference.

I should say that binoculars are essential! Tah and I had settled down as inconspicuously as we could, on a rock, in the midst of an obviously sophisticated group. We watched them for awhile. We strained our eyes in the direction called out from time to time: "There's one at two o'clock and five degrees above the horizon, just over that clump of green!" I could find two o'clock and the five degrees above the horizon and the green clump; but I couldn't spot the hawk or the eagle without high-powered glasses. This went on for perhaps a half-hour, with six or eight sightings soaring across the sky at various points on the imaginary clock and various degrees above the horizon. Eventually a lull set in. Then I noticed a lone bird soaring gracefully above the horizon about fifteen degrees, coursing towards Lookout Rock where we were all seated expectantly. And no one called out that he was there. I felt a compulsion to perform a professional bird-watching duty. So I rendered a well-modulated call: "At one o'clock and fifteen degrees above the horizon—there's one!" And I pointed to emphasize the direction in case I had misused the code.

There was a dead silence. It was clear to me that my call had been faulty. Our immediate neighbors—save one—glanced in the direction of one o'clock and then nonchalantly turned away to look through their glasses in some other direction. The one exception, our nearest neighbor leaned over towards me as he lowered his binoculars. In a stage whisper he said, "A vulture." I slumped in between two boulders and lost interest in the whole profession.

Appalachia:
Where many people
have found the secret
of making a way of life

Tah and I took off Wednesday afternoon for a leisurely hike, with our backpacks prepared for two to three days and nights in the game and bear sanctuary of the North Carolina Wild Life Preserve in the Pisgah. We planned to start at Devil Fork Gap and hike south to Allen Gap.

The day was windy and the countryside was rugged. As we drove north of Asheville, we paralleled the French Broad River, which flows through Appalachia. Wilma Dykeman in her book "The French Broad"* tells the story of the people of Appalachia. In the introduction, she says:

> "The landscape changes. The mountains remain. Many of the people do not. Certain counties of the French Broad Region decreased in population during the past ten years. Natives went elsewhere in search of a livelihood while outlanders came here in search of refuge from the urban blight. It is one of the ironies, and perhaps one of the hopes, of much of Appalachia that many of its people have found the secret of making a way of life where they often could not find means of making a living."

The country is sparsely settled. The few open and comparatively flat areas were planted in vegetable gardens and in patches of tobacco, burned by a recent frost. Tobacco is grown for cash and vegetables for canning to assure food for the table year-round.

We entered the Trail in Shelton country, at Devil Fork Gap, and marched up the hill in that elegant six-foot lane formed by parallel fences. By definition, when you start a hike at a gap on the Appalachian Trail, you start with a climb up a hill. With such a beginning, and your backpack at its heaviest point, the first few minutes seem cruel and unfair, but you know that it's temporary and worth it. The offset will be the descent to the gap at the exit.

Our first night at the Locust Ridge Lean-to was spent with six young men, who arrived from the south singly or in pairs between six and seven o'clock. We were there earlier. Two of the youngsters came from Iowa; they had just graduated and had started hiking the Trail at Springer, Georgia. The others, from Michigan, Indiana and New York, had also started at Springer. They had joined as a group along the way and planned to hike about a month. During the three weeks they'd been together, they had built up quite a camaraderie. They kidded and joked with each other and shared a specialty dish each evening, taking turns innovating. The one from New York wore a Stony Brook tee shirt and had just graduated from college. He was frustrated looking for a teaching job. "For every vacancy in New York, there were

*Published by Holt Rhinehart & Winston Inc., 1955, pp. vi and vii.

350 applicants," he said. He would have liked to move to the southeast if he could get a job. He had hitched rides to Springer.

Doug, the last arrival, was from Grand Rapids, Michigan. He worked in a butcher shop. This was the third time he had come down to hike on the Appalachian Trail. His father dropped him off at Springer, but he planned to hike only two weeks at a time. He "gets lonely and wants to be with the family oftener." He was the last arrival because he hiked more slowly than the others; he had a bum leg, torn muscles. He likes to smoke cigars, one a day after dinner. The others banned him from the camp to smoke. He was allowed to smoke in privacy in the toilet.

The two from Iowa had just graduated from the University, one in the top rung and the other "back in the pack." The latter had turned down an appointment to West Point because he preferred the Air Force Academy, which appointment he had thought was on the way. He was hiking the trail to get hold of himself after failing to get the Air Force appointment.

Each of them had a small gas stove and a cooking pot which also served as an eating dish. They smeared the bottom of the pot with detergent to prevent blackening.

This segment of the Trail did not appear to be as popular as the Great Smoky Mountains National Park. The six young men told us that last week the Smokies were unbelievably crowded; the trails were like a city sidewalk. In a hard rain and soaked, they had been denied access to a shelter by a pack of Boy Scouts.

We got going Thursday morning at eight-thirty and landed at the Jerry Cabin Lean-to at one-thirty p.m., after three rest stops and lunch. What a great feeling! We had the whole afternoon to laze around!

The luxurious event of the day was a bath by the spring. The forest rangers had installed a fifty-yard length of rubber hose from the spring up-hill to a half of a fifty-five gallon steel drum. The cool water collected in the overflowing drum, providing plenty of clear fresh water to dip from, to splash over the body. It's not often that you can strip by the spring and have enough water to soap and rinse fully. A real pleasure!

The camp site was ours alone. We put on clean clothes, had cocktails, and took a walk, yes, a walk in the woods! Afterwards, we took a nap before dinner. That night I slept so soundly that

On cold nights, we wore our hats to bed.

Tah could not awaken me when a mouse and a woodchuck paid a call on us, rustling around among our paper plates, napkins and soaking breakfast cereal—all stored away on the beam under the eaves of the lean-to.

Friday morning we found the Trail so flat and well laid out that we arrived at Little Laurel Lean-to, after six and a half miles, for lunch at twelve-thirty p.m. Tah led and set a good pace, until suddenly she stopped and I caught up with her. She said, "I just saw a bear! A little one—a cub—crossed the Trail just twenty steps ahead!" I said that we should move on up so that we could see him again. Tah wasn't afraid of the cub; but what about the mother? She must be nearby!

She relinquished the lead to me for a while. We moved on, but did not see the cub again, or the mother. There were signs about every quarter mile along this segment of the Trail, "North Carolina—Wild Life—Game Lands." Some signs announced "Bear Sanctuary." The only other animals we saw were occasional squirrels and chipmunks. There were no signs of wild boar in these parts. We did see deer hoof marks now and again.

After lunch on Friday, just as we decided to move on, a thunderstorm moved in and lasted about twenty minutes. Our boots got wet on the way out, but we were in our car by three p.m. Except for a couple of short ascents, the rest of the way was steadily downhill.

It was a pleasure to hike such well-maintained and considerately laid out trails, and to see the enormous thickets of rhododendrons, the expansive views, especially of the Tennessee Valley as we broke out onto a bald or a point. I blessed the person who switched back the Trail frequently up the mountains, or better yet, who so often led the hiker around the peaks over the brow, instead of over every peak. The foresters had felled trees across the Trail at strategic points to prevent vehicles (especially motorcycles) from encroaching on the Trail.

We thoroughly enjoyed the trip.

Welcome
is a
wonderful
word

The Hostel is what puts Hot Springs, North Carolina on the map of through-hikers of the Appalachian Trail. That's Tah trekking up the main drag looking as though she needed a helping hand. And she is getting one, above, as she arrives at the Hot Springs Campers' Hostel.

Services are offered out of the "Kindness of: Catholic Chapel of the Redeemer." It is run by the Jesuits. Significantly, the sign welcoming trail hikers offers "Free Lodging - for 1 or 2 nights."

A friendly welcome to The Place by Charles Trivett.

Joe McClosky, who showed us around the Hostel, explained the 1 or 2 night limit by pointing out that man has territorial instincts. After a couple of days he claims certain areas and things as his own even though he is a guest. Therefore, it's better for all that no one take up extended residence.

We found that things were tough in the Appalachian community. The unemployment rate was above 20% and there was a scarcity of free-flowing money around town. There was no high school for the teenagers; they had to be bused daily over twenty miles away to a neighboring town for school. The only cafe in town had been closed. The motel was in poor shape; all but one of its television sets were not working. The owner had stopped replacing burned-out light bulbs.

All of this was at contrast with the vigor we had observed just two years earlier, when the motel was functioning well and the Henderson Cafe was moderately busy, even though Doug Norton, the owner, did find time to do some logging also.

The AT follows the main street through town and across the French Broad River on U.S. Routes 70 and 25.

Not long after crossing the Tennessee-Virginia line, the northbound hiker finds himself on the main street of Damascus, Virginia. The Trail runs through the middle of the town where three names have become familiar to all through hikers: Grindstaff, Trivett and Sprinkle.

Paschal Grindstaff is the Postmaster; Charles and Alice Trivett are volunteer overseers of The Place; and Reverend Ken Sprinkle is the pastor of the Methodist Church which turned a vacant house behind the church into a hostel called The Place. They are all friends of the hikers and provide free, or for donations, a place to rest and sleep and a place to cook and shower. The Place has two large upstairs dormitories with mattresses, which give the hiker a chance to return to civilization and its amenities after a month of walking from Springer, Georgia. He cooks on his own stove, but he has the use of a refrigerator, hot showers, and nearby supply stores and a laundry.

Best of all, the hospitable overseers offer the hikers more than physical amenities; they offer friendship, companionship, advice and assistance if needed. Many hikers write in the Trail registers that The Place is a welcome highlight of the Trail experience.

We had heard of Graymoor monastery from Mrs. Marcinak on our first hike on the AT. It is a short hike north of the Hudson River Bridge. When we first heard of it, it did not mean much to us, as we were only beginners and only day hikers. Later we visited Graymoor because we had heard of it so often from hikers. We found it to be a top-drawer welcome haven for "Appalachian Trail Travelers." Brother John welcomed us and conducted us on a complete tour of the monastery.

At Harpers Ferry, the ATC really came alive

This is Jean Cashin, welcoming Tah to the Appalachian Trail Conference headquarters in Harpers Ferry, West Virginia. As you can see from Tah's expression, this is a nice place to visit. And an easy one, too—only one mile west of the Trail.

Harpers Ferry is a landmark town of great historical significance during early colonial days as well as Civil War times. Today, the town is the mecca to all Appalachian Trail hikers. The Appalachian Trail Conference headquarters there and the most helpful communications about the Trail are issued therefrom. The ATC is the clearinghouse and coordinator for activities having to

do with the Trail from Springer to Katahdin. It provided the leadership to get the Trail designated as a National Scenic Trail in 1968. Then in 1978, it was influential in a most important piece of federal legislation, the funding of up to $90 million over three years to acquire land or rights-of-way to provide a suitable corridor for the Trail. This program is to eliminate conflicts of interest between Trail locations and private owners or developers. It will also permit the Trail to be relocated off public highways to more desirable locations.

To know the Trail is to know a lot of America

The vast sprawl and variety of the American landscape comes home to you as you hike the Appalachian Trail. One day you're driving to the Trail through serene stretches of rural Virginia (above) near Wytheville. Another, you as a hiker are the main thing on Main Street in small town America.

The Trail in Connecticut was a sentimental journey—it seems like yesterday, but it was in 1941 that Tah and I honeymooned at Candlewood Lake, near New Milford, Connecticut and near the Trail.

It was a sentimental journey

Our fondest recollections of western Connecticut revolved around our honeymoon at Candlewood Lake, near New Milford in 1941. We had hiked short segments of the Appalachian Trail during our two weeks at Candlewood, but without any idea of ever hiking the whole thing!

The Trail leaves New York and crosses into Connecticut at Schaghticoke Mountain, between Webatuck and Kent. It traverses the Taconic Range and the Housatonic Valley in western Connec-

ticut. After fifty-five miles in Connecticut, it crosses into
Massachusetts in Sage's Ravine, an outstandingly beautiful spot.
The Trail crosses the Housatonic River, first, on Cornwall Bridge
and again just west of Falls Village. We enjoyed three overnights
at The White Hart Inn in Salisbury.

The Trail runs through South Canaan, near Norfolk, where I
spent two pleasant summers at the country club as "Tennis Professional" in 1939 and 1940. Weekends I courted Tah at Butler

Hospital in Providence, R.I., where she was in training while in Yale School of Nursing, or when she came to Candlewood occasionally.

When we dropped off Mt. Algo and approached Connecticut Highway 341, I began to hark back to pre-World War II and the autumn after the war years when as a coach with Hopkins Grammar School athletic teams in New Haven, I came to the playing fields of Kent School. Those were the days of Graduate School at Yale "and we thought they'd never end!"

We backpacked into Macedonia State Park and spent a night in the Chase Mountain Lean-to. It was on the way out to Housatonic River Road the next day that we sat on some ledges, taking a ten-minute rest break. A babble of voices floated up to us from below, the sounds of children laughing and parents urging caution and restraint. There was something familiar about the goings-on. Could it be–? Yes, possibly it could be our son Bob and his family, Lucy, Betsy and Jesse! They had hiked in to surprise us at St. John's Ledges!

The Trail in Massachusetts continues on a northward course for eighty-four miles into somewhat higher elevations between Sage's Ravine at the Connecticut-Massachusetts line and the Vermont line three miles above Blackinton.

Whereas Connecticut hills are mainly under 2,000 feet and its highest is 2,316 feet (Bear Mountain near Sage's Ravine), the Trail in Massachusetts traversed four peaks over 2,900 feet between Cheshire and Blackinton: Saddle Ball Mountain (3,239 feet), Mt. Greylock (3,491 feet), Mt. Finch (3,110 feet), and Mt. Williams (2,951 feet).

At South Egremont, Massachusetts college kids working in the Jug End Resort recreational programs were happy to shuttle hikers in the hotel van. (Jugend, German for "youth," was a youth center built for early German settlers. Today, the word Jugend has been Americanized and the resort, pictured below, is known as Jug End.) We made arrangements at the desk and they assigned Liz to drive for us. She was studying voice in preparation for what she hoped would be a career as a mezzo soprano in opera.

Hikers don't only hike

Tah is a painter—a water-colorist. Every year at April 15 I get a kick out of filling in the "Occupation of Spouse" blank with the word *Artist*. It rings with a much better tone than *Wife*.

She has been interested in art since childhood. Her grandparents on both sides had achieved some renown as painters in Austria. But she couldn't get around to committing the time, energy and discipline to art while being a full-time wife of one and mother of four. Spare time from cooking, scrubbing, changing diapers and snow-suits, and attending PTA meetings had to be given to entertaining visiting firemen or my business associates or clients. And when we had multiple servants in Puerto Rico—one

or two for tending children, one for cooking, one for house cleaning, and one for laundry—Tah still had no spare time. She spent
all her time tending to the problems of the servants. Nap time for
the children gave her no time off, either. The servants needed her.
With all that, she had no time to respond to the urge for art.

Once the children were away at school, or had flown the nest,
she signed up for the regular Tuesday sessions of Ed Whitney at
the Bronx Botanical Gardens in New York. Ed was teaching water-
color, at which there is none better. He is recognized as an
outstanding painter and teacher, a rare combination. Ed did
wonders for Tah, as he does for anyone who studies with him. He

believes that art is an expression of an individual person and the medium is for the sole purpose of serving that individual expression. There are as many styles as there are individual painters. However, he propounds certain principles of design which are common to all media and to all painters. Within the framework of a few fundamentals, he teaches an artist "how to" express himself or herself most freely and effectively.

It's striking that, with his insistence—or rather persistent encouragement—that his students express themselves in their own way and in their own spirit; an Ed Whitney student can recognize another Ed Whitney student by merely seeing the student's work.

Zoltan Szabo, a native of Hungary, emigrated to Canada at age 21 in 1949. He has achieved an international reputation in water-color techniques and especially in landscape painting. He is of great benefit to beginning as well as advanced artists in that he leaves nothing in doubt about technique, including how to use sprinkled salt onto a wet wash to create star-like shapes imitating snow.

His latest book sports a couple of paragraphs on "Happy Accidents," how he not only looks for but tries to manipulate accidents which add spontaneity to water colors!

Zoltan Szabo and Ed Whitney would certainly agree on "happy accidents" as a good thing. And it seemed to me that Tah could benefit from both teachers; as different as they are, they do not seem to be at odds. Anyway, what she really needed more than anything else was opportunity and discipline. Therefore, I encouraged her to take a week's break from the Trail in Manchester Depot, Vermont and go with twenty others to Szabo's class.

While she was painting, I went home to Tryon, N.C. to check on things there. She would not be completely alone among strangers in Manchester, because Vivian Smith, a long-time friend from Westford, Massachusetts, was also in the class. They had a ball!

When I returned to Manchester, Tah and I thoroughly enjoyed visiting the Southern Vermont Art Center. For her birthday present I gave her a membership in the Art Center which has become an inducement for her to offer some of her paintings for showing and for sale.

Southern Vermont Art Center, Manchester, Vermont.

J & T
Flack
slept
here

We stayed at some marvelously interesting places, including the Melody Inn, shown with owner Elmer Johnson and dog, above. Tah found such places good copy for letters home.

Dear Family:

When we were in Vermont last week, Dad said that if we could find a motel in or near the small town of Danby,

that would be close to if not the ideal central location for
us the next two nights. Danby is a town of fewer than 500;
actually it calls itself a settlement. It is off the main road.
Luckily, there was a sign "Melody Inn" right next to THE
store: post office, drug counter and antique store all rolled
into one. The description of the inn you will not believe.
Here was a gorgeous, immense Victorian mansion intact,

with a Swiss chalet addition tacked onto its side. Quite an architectural wonder, to say the least. The story behind this building is particularly interesting.

Silas Griffith imported French Canadian and Italian loggers and workers into the mills, which practice was not readily accepted by the local Vermonters. He gave credit to his workers in his local store and often cancelled $200 and $300 debts in bursts of generosity.

He was usually quite generous. He set up $20,000 in a trust fund with the purpose of buying Christmas presents in perpetuity for children in the town of Danby. He left money for a library and a trust fund to provide clothes for the needy.

In the 1890's, Silas Griffith became Vermont's first millionaire—lumbering, and also manufacturing charcoal. He had this huge mansion built for himself and his family. The outside is a typically large Victorian mansion; behind it is a tremendous carriage house; he must have had at least eight carriages in there. There were five family bedrooms upstairs in front, four servants' bedrooms upstairs in back. On the first floor, there were three living rooms (parlors), a dining room, a kitchen, a butler's pantry and two servants' quarters behind the kitchen. The wainscotting was all in curly maple; the wooden door and window frames, as well as the fireplaces, were gorgeous curly maple, in the Biddemeier style, as well as the banisters, etc. The fireplaces had Italian tiles. You get the picture, all very elegant and in high fashion of the day. There is a Griffith Lake and a Griffith Memorial Library (in a town of 500!!!). Apparently, he got angry at the Vermonters for some reason; or they got angry with him as he hired French Canadians to lumber for cheaper wages than he'd have to pay the local inhabitants. At any rate, he left Vermont in a huff and had a replica of this house built on the west coast. There is a Silas Griffith Park in Los Angeles, we are told.

The house at Danby was sold and now it is a hunting lodge. Elmer Johnson bought it and runs it as a "hunting and fishing lodge." He made a huge dining room in the carriage house, where he can, if necessary, feed up to 100 people. Upstairs in the carriage house he can sleep thirty hunters in double rooms. He used to be a contractor-builder and it is his own design and idea to tack on the

Swiss chalet addition to the main house. The original house can sleep up to thirty-five, plus the dormitory in the attic which sleeps thirteen. The addition has about six rooms opening up onto the porch.

When we got there, we had the whole house to ourselves. The old dining room had been converted into a ping-pong and pool room; the lower part of the addition had been made into a huge lounge with fireplace. We had the three parlors, the kitchen, eight bathrooms and untold bedrooms to ourselves for the price of one room, namely, $15.00. I doubt that he makes a lot of money but he really enjoys life; he makes a lot of friends who return every year. And he goes hunting and fishing with them. Weekends, of course, the place is usually quite full. Fortunately, we were there during the week. He's a very outgoing, relaxed man who loves to talk to and meet people, but he is completely without a sense of cohesion of architectural styles; he loves every bit of old wood and tiles in the place; he appreciates the old. With great pride he showed us the stained glass windows and how he personally repaired one of them.

We are at Karen's and Tom's today, having arrived last night. One week and we will be home again—we both are in excellent shape from the hiking; at least we feel good. We also tend to *droop* at 9 p.m. as we have been rising at 5 a.m. (can you believe it—it's the truth, tho) when we are at motels.

We have hiked 264 miles on this trip so far...we lack forty some odd miles to finish off the northeast. We have just finished Vermont.

Karen's calling. Got to go.

Love, Me.

The truck-stops along the throughways paralleling the Appalachian Trail were welcome sights to us. These are generally located for the convenience of truckers and they also served our convenience. Their motel rooms are consistently clean and comfortable and they provide twenty-four-hour service at the gas pumps and in the restaurant. For the professional drivers, the truck-stops provided game and TV rooms as well as showers and towels. Most importantly, complete services for the 18-wheelers were provided. For us the convenience of meals at all hours, especially breakfast at four-thirty or five a.m., was most attractive.

We did not come to know the truck-drivers personally. Nevertheless, we thought that we could identify the type anywhere at any time. Characteristically, he has a huge pot; his trousers hang low on his hips; in warm weather he wears an undershirt, but no outershirt; and he is a chain cigarette smoker. He is a most respectful and skilled truck maneuverer. He is reliable and safe on the highway. And he is such a good pace-setter that he is a pleasure to follow on long distances on through-ways.

We especially enjoyed our three-night stay in the truckstop at Frystown, Pennsylvania and our four-night stay at Cloverdale, Virginia.

The Quality Inn at Summerdale, a few minutes south and west of Harrisburg, Pennsylvania, was a most enjoyable five-day stay when we were hiking the Trail in the vicinity. Eddie Allen, one of the owners of the Inn, was in the lobby as I checked in. He overheard me say that my wife would not stay the second night as she planned to drive to Swarthmore College for her class reunion but would return for the third, fourth and fifth nights. He introduced himself and wished to send greetings to Lew Elverson, the Athletic Director and former head football coach at Swarthmore. Eddie had known Lew when they both played football together at the University of Pennsylvania and had coached small colleges in competition with each other for many years.

The Quality Inn at Summerdale measured up to the usually high standards of this chain of good motels. In addition it offered a bit extra in the way of atmosphere and food. The motif of railroading ran throughout the place; rooms were named after railroads present and past; one of the dining rooms was a dining car from a passenger train. It had been carefully mounted on heaving springs which permitted the room to sway as people walked through it. Pictures of well-known engines and railroad cars hung on the walls throughout the restaurant. Furthermore, a short distance across the highway out front was a huge switching yard for freight trains to be made up or resorted. The sounds of cars being "humped" were music to the ears of the railroad buff.

Choose your own dining spot—a cozy indoor retreat, or Mother Nature's Trail Tearoom.

In the Shenandoah, the A.T. is an elegant footpath

We loved the Shenandoah National Park in Virginia so much that we saved the last thirty-three miles of the Trail to finish there. We enjoyed staying in the Big Meadows Lodge.

Steve Kettler was the desk clerk at Big Meadows in the fall of 1978. He checked us in when we went there in September to hike four days south of the Lodge to complete the Appalachian Trail. He had agreed to shuttle us daily before he had to go on duty. On

the fourth day he apologized to us for having been so reserved the first couple of rides. And then he opened up with some searching questions about our relationship with nature. He said that he had observed how thoughtful and considerate we were towards wildlife. (We had merely driven slowly and given right of way to gamboling, white-tailed deer in the park.) His direct question was "Do you feel closer to God while walking in the wilderness?"

My reply was to the effect that we may not feel closer, but, more importantly, we see constant evidences and reminders that He is present. Even if we may differ among ourselves as to who or what He is, we cannot but affirm the presence of an overall power, intelligence, supreme being, god or God. The immensity and awesomeness, and dependability and predictability, the absolutely neutral character of the natural world and universe are completely convincing. It is regrettable that sects and partisan groups so often so narrowly claim superiority in the name of their dogma, their

119

Allah, their Gods. It's a marvel that human beings don't abandon narrow, power-hungry religious sects and completely return to nature.

We continue to marvel at the contrast between before-and-after appearances of this 300-square-mile spread of ridges of the Shenandoah National Park. Here is a refreshing case of local citizens and state government, with a vision, restoring farmed-out ridge lands to forests. They jointly raised the money to buy the land and then turned it over to the Federal government to develop and care for as a park. Between 1924 and 1935 some 24,000 citizens raised one and a quarter million dollars and the State of Virginia put up a million dollars to acquire the land. The once barren hills are today covered with forests which provide beautiful homes for wild animals, including deer in great numbers, opossums, raccoons, black bears, rabbits, skunks, bob cats, turkeys, foxes and squirrels. The park also provides a course

through which the Skyline Drive meanders. Along side it, but off to itself, is the Appalachian Trail, now maintained by the dedicated members of the Potomac Appalachian Trail Club (PATC).

This segment of the Trail is the most elegant footpath conceivable. Even the curves are banked! Most of it was constructed by the Civilian Conservation Corps (CCC) in the midst of the Great Depression of the 1930's. This is one of those public projects to create jobs for the unemployed which was of truly great and lasting benefit to the republic! I salute them every time I think of their contribution. We feel that the Shenandoah National Park provided an appropriate element of elegance to the Appalachian Trail. We expect to return there at regular intervals for the rest of our lives!

Further to the north, the AMC (Appalachian Mountain Club) does a good job of coping while maintaining their cool. They are constantly devising ways to make the mountain and wilderness experience more enjoyable for the hordes who come to their area (eastern Pennsylvania through northern New Hampshire). At the same time, they struggle to prevent the users from destroying their environment. This requires heavy doses of education and steady imposition of control. Their education programs are persuasive to members who read their output. AMC learned sometime ago that it takes discipline to assure control.

"CARRY IN----CARRY OUT" (litter) or "PACK IT IN----PACK IT OUT" has been advertised or sloganized persistently by the U.S. Forest Service and the AMC. And along with it frequent and repeated publication of the alternative methods of handling waste has begun to have a positive effect. This simple instruction has a ring of sincerity and straight-forwardness; it commands respect. Somewhat in contrast to this is a less effective bit of insouciance in a guidebook for the Shenandoah: "The candy bar you take into the woods should provide at least the energy for bringing the wrapper out."

It took many years for the AMC and other mountain clubs to find the best way to preserve the fragile bogs along the Trail. Continued research, testing and experimentation will go on and perhaps an even better "best" way will be found. The most recent seemed to be the laying of two logs parallel and end-to-end with other combinations of two logs, each pair spiked together with a cross-piece. The upper sides of the logs are adzed to provide a flat surface, which makes it easy for the hiker to keep his footing. This system is working; the hiker feels that his welfare and comfort are being well served, and that's true. More importantly the fragile bog and its environment are being preserved. There's no temptation to wander off to the right or left in search of a better route, as was the case when stones or single logs were scattered through the bog.

So far the AMC seems to have resisted the temptation and pressures to become a big-time lobbyist organization for conservation causes wherever they might be. They appeal to their members to make their voices heard on clear policies and positions where the club has a direct interest. They do not yet have a cadre of "professionals'' making a career of ''girding up for the big battles'' for causes all over the country and especially before Congress. Many AMC members are hoping that the club will stick to its knitting, conserving and maintaining the natural resources in its own areas for its own membership. Andrew Livingston Nichols, AMC's 74th President, was quoted in *Appalachia,* February, 1977, ''If somebody said '...we should deliberately set out to be, within the limits of law, a lobbying organization,' I would say, 'No, I don't think so.' If there is an issue in which we have a direct interest and expertise, we almost have, within the scope of our objectives, an obligation to do that (lobby). At the same time, to say that our objectives include the license to go out looking for such kinds of things, no, I don't think that's what the AMC has traditionally been, and I don't think it should be.''

On the Trail, you're a guest!

We elected to hike the Trail in the fall of 1976 from Franconia Notch to Pinkham Notch, hut to hut, after Labor Day, because the heavy summer traffic declines as schools begin to reopen and families pack out to return home. Our reservations

124

were made well in advance for each of the huts, eliminating the need to lug a tent. We were extremely lucky with the weather; we had only one day of rain.

The Appalachian Trail in New Hampshire between Franconia Notch and Pinkham Notch has to be classed as one of the super experiences in hiking. It may not be the most demanding; it tries hard not to be. Much of the fifty-mile distance is above tree line and exposed to harsh weather conditions at all times of the year. Frequent warning signs urge hikers to turn back to safety if weather is threatening. The Presidential Range of Mountains has over the years been a magnetic attraction to hordes of people seeking outdoor recreation. Much tramping in the mountains, along the same paths, and unregulated camping wore the wilderness areas pretty badly. The AMC has installed research, experimentation and discipline and it is most rewarding to see and read about the effectiveness of their efforts in cooperation with the U.S. Forest Service.

The AMC over the last ninety of its 102 years has built nine huts a day's hike apart in the White Mountains of New Hampshire. These are full-service huts, open only in the summer and early fall. From an issue of *Appalachia* we learn that some 45,000 guests are fed and housed each year and they consume 200,000 pounds of food. Helicopters fly in the staples, propane gas, and repair supplies, and they haul away the waste, including human waste in 55-gallon drums which act as receptacles when installed in the toilets. Still, each hut-person (some are female) lugs 3,000 pounds of food and supplies every summer.

We were hiking up the trail from Crawford Notch to the AMC Mizpah Spring Hut when we overtook two hutmen, resting midway. They had heavy supply packs on their backs, with ropes lashing huge boxes onto the ladder-back carriers. I asked them whether they would not be happy to have a cable car system installed between the valley and the hut to lug those heavy loads up. Together they said, almost in one voice, "No. We like it the way it is." I asked a puzzled "Why?" Their simple answer was quite revealing of the spirit of the people of the AMC: "Look at how the character of Mt. Washington changed when the cog railway was built!" The hutmen would rather do the drudgery than spoil the primeval aura of their area.

126

The Trail is a robust song—with sometime dissonant notes

The Trail through Delaware Water Gap is on the open road—and drowned by the roaring of 18-wheelers.

Sometimes Nature
takes a back seat

ontana Village, once a robust frontier construction village built in 1946 to house workers constructing the TVA dam on Little Tennessee River, lies just outside the southwest corner of the Great Smoky Mountains National Park. It is a delightful and welcome interlude for hikers. It is now run by Government Services, Inc. as a recreation center, with primitive to luxury accommodations.

The Great Smoky Mountains National Park has become more and more crowded. It is estimated that one-half (over 100 million) of the population of the United States lives within one day's automobile drive of the Park! And more people are hiking and picnicing each year. It has the distinction of having more visitors annually than any other national park. We first hiked the park in May, 1972, from Newfound Gap to Cades Cove. (See "Later we worried that one bear had read the sign," page 10.) We did receive a fire permit, but no reservations for shelters were required, even though the guide book said they were advisable. We returned to complete the Park in May, 1976, and found that reservations for specific shelters were strictly required and even then there was no guarantee of space. The "committed" through-hikers from Springer to Katahdin were required to have reservations for shelters in general only. I guess the theory was that they could not predict precisely which shelter they needed on a given night.

In the Smokies, the violent thunderstorms frequently occur late in the afternoon, often about the time the hiker is still scrambling to reach shelter. He has a double incentive to reach these solidly built shelters, as the one in Davenport Gap: both as a shelter from storms as well as from prowling bears.

In the Glenwood District of Jefferson National Forest the ice storms of a month earlier (April, 1978) caused much damage. The storms literally raised havoc in forests above 2,000 feet elevation; huge oak and maple limbs were broken and strewn across the Trail, which had only been partially cleared by forest crewmen. Locust trees at all altitudes had been shattered. Where they grew in groves, it looked as though a tornado had struck and ripped the tops out of them. Even young pines were broken from their tops down and many were uprooted. Crews had been very busy keeping the Blue Ridge Parkway open.

The Trail between Petite's Gap and Snowden on the James River is described in the guide book as "a magnificent walk." We agree. It was a day of mountain laurel, rattlesnake plantain, galax and Solomon's-seal. Here and there were blue, blue spider wort. We enjoyed the mountain laurel especially between 2,000 and 3,000 feet elevation. It was in full flower; we have never seen such full bloom! A veritable flower land!

On our hike between Cornelius Creek Lean-to and Middle Creek-North Creek Road we ran into noise pollution of a high intensity. It sounded like high tension electric lines. I felt like writing a letter of protest to the Virginia Electric Power Company. Little good it would have done. We finally discerned from someone else it was a horde of locusts invading the region!*

On that same day we met Scott Steiner, a through-hiker, who planned to finish by mid-August to return to the University of Maryland. He had already hiked from Katahdin south to Massachusetts. To make time he had stripped his pack, no rain gear, no extra shoes, no tent or tarp. He had to face only one night without a shelter all the way to Waynesboro. If it rained or threatened rain, he planned to hike on after dark and sleep during the day. He planned to go twenty-six miles that day.

Scott said that many hikers he'd met class Stekoah in North Carolina as the toughest part of the Trail. He believed the Bigelows in Maine are the hardest to hike. Tah thinks the Mahoosuc Mountains of Maine are the toughest.

What does one do if he hikes into a forest fire just beginning? We faced this one Sunday afternoon while hiking the Trail in New York's Harriman State Park between Arden Mountain and Tiorati Brook Road. A careless camper had pitched his tent near the Trail on a brook. His campfire had spread to dry grasses and leaves. About an acre had already burned when we arrived. The camper was nowhere in sight. We yanked his tent loose from its pegs and

---

*Although these clear-winged and noisy insects are locally called locusts, they are really periodic cicadas, which return on a seventeen-year cycle. Shortly after birth the cicada digs its way into the ground where it first drops. It stays underground for seventeen years, sucking sap from the roots of plants until it's time to emerge. The cicada deposits eggs in slits which it bores, generally into fruit tree twigs. "When the weakened twigs mature into fruit-bearing limbs, they break under the weight of the fruit, and the crop is lost. Failure of this sort can be avoided by not planting young fruit trees in years of cicada emergence." (Encyclopaedia Britannica, 1976, Vol. 8, p. 1036.)

saved it from burning and then proceeded to thrash the grass blazes on the down-wind side with green brushes made of limbs from small bushes. After an hour of this, a group of fifteen day-hikers came by and joined us. When the fire appeared to be coming under some control we proceeded on our hike, depending upon the local hiker-residents to manage it.

The Appalachian Trail crosses the Mason-Dixon line separating Maryland and Pennsylvania. From Pen Mar to the Susquehanna River is 80 miles; the Trail to Delaware Water Gap covers another 140 miles for a total of 220 miles in Pennsylvania.

The crossing of the Cumberland Valley on the AT from South Mountain to the Susquehanna River at Duncannon is through fertile and practically level farmlands, and on too many miles of public highways.

Farms in the Cumberland Valley are accented with silos and large barns surrounded by cornfields and cover crops. In early spring the odor is cow manure, spread on the fields before being plowed. Crows, blackbirds and pigeons, a few robins and some kingfishers roam the fields for worms and insects.

North of Duncannon the Trail is generally on a ridge of the Alleghenies at the 1,400 to 1,500-foot level, with intermediate gaps and cuts through which run the streams and roads. So it is up and down on the Trail between 500 and 1,500 feet for 140 miles, with rock outcroppings increasing in frequency and size as the Trail proceeds north. Finally at Eckville the outcroppings become so intense, the hiker cannot take his eyes off the spot for his next step.

By the time we got to Swatara Gap we were getting a bit tired of the rocks. It seemed that we were endlessly on them, all day, eyes down, constantly watching where to put our feet. We had been told that Pennsylvania was rocky, hard on the feet and worse on the boots. "Pennsylvania will tear up a good pair of boots," we were cautioned.

Tah grumbled. But she consoled herself that we were already north of Eckville which the guidebook had warned was the most unpleasant rock area. At lunch she wanted to know how much more of this unpleasantness we had to endure. An ominous, dead

silence overlay us after I read aloud that Eckville was better than
sixty miles ahead of us. We had not yet reached the difficult part.

Except in state forests, the rocky land of southern Pennsylvania is sparsely covered with scrub oak. Was it thinned by the
charcoal and iron industry? Or is the land so poor it won't grow
more and larger trees? Probably the answer is some of both, plus
out-of-control fires in the distant past. The area is obviously
popular for recreation, with camp sites and picnic areas galore and
fishing streams one after another both in state game forests and
private lands.

We were struck by the incidence of "For Sale" signs posted
on real estate along the highways between Lehigh River and
Delaware Water Gap. It seemed that the whole countryside was
for sale.

To our friend, Jean Boutilier, in Tryon, who migrated from
Pennsylvania to North Carolina, we said, "Pennsylvania is very
friendly to hikers, except for the mosquitoes, timber rattlesnakes,
rock outcroppings and poison ivy!" On one occasion I stepped
over a timber rattlesnake, coiled among the rocks, without my seeing it and fortunately without his striking. Tah froze when she saw
it as she came along a few steps behind me. I reluctantly killed it
because, as Tah said, "He was a threat to the Boy Scouts."

Despite these nuisances, the Trail in Pennsylvania is a grand
challenge.

135

Sometimes it's better to escape to shelter

The Susquehanna Shelter is about a mile up the ridge from the Susquehanna River after a trail crossing of a railroad and busy highway on the east side of the river. Some person had written in the register at the shelter of his disillusionment. He had arrived late in the afternoon and discovered that the noise of the train and truck traffic below was quite disturbing. To avoid this he had packed out and climbed to the top of the mountain to spread his blanket and hopefully to sleep in peace and quiet. However, not long after dark, the weather turned and heavy showers with thunder and lightning frightened him into retreating to the shelter below. After a hazardous retreat, he wrote, he concluded that it is sheer hyprocrisy for man to try to escape from civilization.

It took nearly a half hour for the storm to pass. It was awesome and beautiful while it lasted!

I have in mind an occurrence in Delaware Water Gap, Pennsylvania. Tah and I had pulled into a service station to get gasoline and to enquire about getting someone to drive us in our car to an entry point on the Appalachian Trail in New Jersey.

I had just completed making arrangements for the niece of the service station owner to drive us at a negotiated price of eight dollars. I so announced this to Tah, who sat in the front seat of our car. She questioned how I had arrived at eight dollars when I had said that six dollars ought to be enough. My answer that the station owner had suggested the eight dollars left a gap in Tah's mind. I judged that she was pressing me too hard and in a show of temper I said that she could negotiate next time. With that I threw the map into the front seat of the car. Unintentionally and most unfortunately, the map struck Tah in the face. She thought it was deliberate.

There's no shelter from some storms

At this point she gave eloquence to the meaning of the word *furious*. And for five minutes it flamed! As I retreated from the car, things started flying from the window onto the parapet of the service station—anything loose she threw, the map, newspaper, notepads, safety-belt (the loose end), as well as punctuating screams. I didn't dare return to apologize a second time until the storm had settled somewhat.

However, the young man standing by the pumps quite calmly went over and collected the debris to deliver it back to the car. He said not a word but conducted himself as though this was a normal activity to which he was accustomed. I interceded and accepted the various pieces with "thanks." What he didn't know was that had he delivered them back to Tah, they would have added fuel to her ferocity. She would have chucked them out again!

Slogging and dodging

Most bogs or lakes or small streams which the Trail crosses in New England are caused by busy beavers. Such crossings are hazardous when the hiker is loaded with a full backpack. We found it most helpful to use two poles to balance while searching for a solid footing.

The trails in the Smokies are subject to storm-felled trees (blowdowns) but park personnel respond quickly and efficiently to restore good grooming. In some sections of Virginia and in Maine, on private lands, response tended to be slow to clean up blowdowns. And in Baxter State Park in Maine, such clean up activity was presumed to have been prohibited in the deed conveying the property to the State. There was a condition that the park land would forever be kept in a natural state. However, the Appalachian Trail does eventually get cleared after blowdowns, even in Baxter State Park.

There's sorrow
in them hills

The Appalachian Trail between Sams Gap and Watauga Dam is a rugged eighty-mile section. It's beautiful but dangerous.

The Roan Mountain is in this section and it is a wonder to behold, especially in June when the rhododendron plants are in full bloom, or in October when the leaves are in full color! We hiked from Iron Mountain Gap through Hughes Gap in June; across Roan Mountain, through Carver's Gap and across Grassy Ridge in October; through Yellow Mountain Gap, Moreland Gap and Dennis Cove in June of the following year. Hiking friends from Tryon, N.C. joined us each time: Betty Frost, Dave and Adie Kirby, Art Nelson, Louise Lamson and Sink and Barbe Manning.

The ten-mile section between Carver's Gap and Route 19E traverses five summits over 5,400 feet with Grassy Ridge in the Roan group rising to 6,189 feet. North from 19E, the Trail goes through Laurel Fork Gorge, accessible only on foot and only by the AT. This gorge is of universal scenic beauty.

As beautiful as the section of the Trail is between Roan Mountain and east of Elizabethton, Tennessee it has the reputation of being dangerous, especially for girls without escorts. It is reported that twenty-two stills for making moonshine whiskey have been demolished by law officers in a recent three-year period in this area.

Four teenage girls from Raleigh, N.C. were robbed and raped by five local, moonshine-drinking men in June, 1978. The criminals were brought to trial and sentenced to ten to fifteen years in jail. A local resident was quoted as saying: "This is a beautiful county. God has blessed it with physical beauty. But I don't know. There's something about the people."

Dot Jackson, a feature writer for The Charlotte Observer, tells the story of the whippoorwill haunting the shelter near Watauga Lake in memory of the murder of Janice Balza from Wisconsin. Janice had gone hiking on the Appalachian Trail alone to celebrate graduation from college in 1975. She met Paul Bigley, a 51-year old Arizona tree surgeon, who joined her for several days of walking. Then one morning at the Vanderventer Lean-to while Janice cooked breakfast Bigley killed her with his hatchet. The shelter from then on has been haunted by the all-night calling of the whippoorwill.

We had been warned but we really didn't believe this story about the all-night, unending song of a whippoorwill. Unfortunately, he was there when we were and he was in full voice. He had little rhythm, just staccato bursts, with persistence and volume, from dark 'til dawn! He kept us awake most of the night. Tah claims he was demented!

Laurel Fork Gorge—most of the
time it was quiet and peaceful.

You never know when the day will end

Tah put her foot down, but for sure, when we hiked all the way out from Congdon Camp in Vermont south to Blackinton, Massachusetts. It took us eleven and a half hours. We arrived as dark fell, and after having to shout at hunters to hold their fire until we passed. Our original plan had been to hike this distance in

two days; but when we arrived at the Seth Warner Shelter at mid-point of the thirteen-mile distance, we found no water readily available in mid-September. We decided to go on since it was only two o'clock. At the end Tah quite properly swore off any more double-digit days, hours or miles. We didn't stick to it, regrettably, as Tah's letter about a later hike demonstrates.

Dear Family - or whoever is home at the moment:

We are in a very small town called Groseclose, next door to Rural Retreat, Virginia—which *is* a retreat. The population is 787! It is in southern Virginia. The AT happens to go right through the town of Groseclose which consists of a motel, a restaurant (reputation for some of the "best home-cooked food") and a gas station. We will spend the night in the motel, having just *emerged* from our first backpack expedition in three months.

We left the car at Big Walker Mountain yesterday at seven a.m. and started walking, each with a backpack, but considerably lighter than usual, as we were going to spend only *one* night in a shelter and did not need more than four meals along.

The shelter was eight miles from our starting point. The beginning was quite steep and tough going, but once up, the ridge trail was lovely, cool and easy. Because we were so far south, the growth was very luxuriant; the trees were tall and full, oak, pine and nut trees. The undergrowth was full, too. However, as a result of the extreme drought and heat this summer, the stream beds were dry. Fortunately, we carried a quart of orange juice, which we had at lunch, saving one cup for later. At two-thirty we arrived at the shelter—good work! Prosit! We did well, we drank the orange juice to celebrate and to quench our terrible thirst as we were both very hot, very sticky, and very wet from the exertion. Jim went to the spring to get more water while I started thinking about unpacking. Jim came back; no water; spring was dry! A note says there is water two and one-half miles down the Trail.

By now it is three o'clock; we are hot, thirsty and tired but we need water to cook dinner. (I brought dry spaghetti,

147

dry tomato sauce, instant soup, instant coffee!) We rest for one-half hour and then start off. What do we hear in the distance? Thunder? Yes! Threatening clouds. Shall we leave the dry shelter and risk getting caught in a thunderstorm? We huddle under a tree (a low one in a grove) for twenty minutes and decide we are too thirsty. We need water. Anyway, the storm seems to be going around us. It did!

After an eternal two hours, rough underfoot, steep downhill hike, Jim and I *stagger,* exhausted, to a creek. There *is* water but it does not look too good. We must *boil* it for twenty minutes before using. It is five-thirty; we pitch

in and start boiling. Jim looks for a place for us to put the sleeping bags; he ties up the tarpaulin over them. How lucky he brought it along! We have only two pots and it takes forever to boil the water. I remember we have halazone tablets along. I drop a couple in the quart of water and then help Jim with unloading. We are *so* thirsty!! After a half hour I say I'm ready to drink the halazone water which is supposed to taste like clorox. I drink long and deeply; it doesn't taste like clorox. I look; the tablets have not dissolved! No wonder! I finally get the spaghetti cooked but we are both too tired to eat much. Soon the boiled water cools enough to drink and the tablets dissolve as well. Also, the flies and mosquitoes which had been thick as thieves, disappeared with the smoke of the fire; our thirst was quenched; we were cooler and felt better. Things looked brighter.

As we crept into our sleeping bags (having hung up the food in bags in the trees), we wondered if we were going to be able to move the next day. We were very sore and stiff. However, having done those extra two and one-half miles of Monday's hike on Sunday, we had only five miles to do the next day. Jim jokingly said it would probably take us all day to do those five miles. Ha! Ha! Well, it took us *nearly* all day. We arrived here at two-thirty; but we are in *one* piece and not quite as sore as we deserved to be. We have a half-day hike scheduled for tomorrow and then we move on to northern Virginia. We are picking up the gaps and sections we had missed this spring. Today is Dad's birthday. We are going out to a spiffy restaurant twenty miles away and have a good steak to celebrate. We *are* having *fun* and soon will be steel and skin—so tough. Last year at this time we were with S&E in White Mountains, remember?

Love to all,

KEF

History is where the hiker finds it

In Civil War country, one never gets very far from history. For example, we hiked Maryland's thirty-nine miles in four days, staying at night in a motel in Hagerstown, enjoying a lunch at South Mountain Inn in Turner's Gap and getting caught up in the history of South Mountain. We sympathized with the distillers who rebelled against the tax on whiskey in 1794.

We became aware of the extensive iron-making industry and its furnaces which had been fed by charcoal made from hardwoods harvested from the hills in the area. The most noted is memorialized in a monument to Thaddeus Stevens, at the entrance to Caledonia State Park off Route 30, Lincoln Highway. His iron works had been demolished during the Gettysburg campaign by the Confederate soldiers.

This monument was erected by the State of Virginia in memory of the troops that fought at Gettysburg. It is located at the spot where General Robert E. Lee watched the "gallant" (read "disastrous") Pickett's Charge into entrenched Union positions resulting in 10,000 casualties out of 15,000 Confederate troops committed to the assault.

VIRGINIA

Echo of Antietam: After the volleys, not a stall

For the three days that we were headquartered in Gettysburg, Pennsylvania, we became deeply immersed in the dominant theme and scene there, the Civil War battle of Gettysburg.

Today it seems fair to ask a question even though we have over a hundred years of hindsight: Whatever possessed the leadership of the Confederate forces to squander so blatantly so many lives at Antietam in 1862 and at Gettysburg in 1863, battles fought less than a year apart? No matter what possessed General Robert E. Lee and/or Jefferson Davis, it seems clear that the judgment behind the decisions was grossly and callously arrogant and naive, a disastrous set of attributes: 24,000 casualties at Antietam followed within a year with 51,000 at Gettysburg! And the fighting was at close quarters, with rifles, bayonets and short-range artillery, with soldiers on foot and a few officers on horseback, principally hanging back in the shade out of range, as was the case of Confederate General Pickett who sent 15,000 men charging into entrenched Union positions. Only one-third survived to retreat!

The failure of General Lee to delay General Pickett's charge until Jeb Stuart's cavalry unit could attack Union forces from the

of corn nor a soldier was left standing here.

rear was a rare error in timing. If he had waited, he would have learned that Jeb Stuart's mission was a failure. Then Pickett's Charge could have been held up or rescheduled with a better chance of success.

The final strategic error was Union General Mead's permitting General Lee to withdraw his battered army to Virginia and prolong the war for nearly two more years.

And we suffered through an attempt at trying to understand and get the feeling of the Battle of Antietam in 1862, which was preceded by the Battle of South Mountain during the early stages of the Civil War. I came away convinced that by failing to win at Antietam the South lost its chance of winning the war, since General Lee's basic mission was to demonstrate that the South could win and hold a position in northern terrritory. If he could have done this the Confederacy would have been assured of help from both France and England. Therefore, Antietam was absolutely crucial, for both sides. The tragedy is that so many casualties occurred in one day, 24,000! And the war dragged on for nearly three more years!

One of the most touching things we saw at Antietam was a cornfield with nothing but stubble on it. Here, on September 17, 1862, Confederate soldiers had hidden between rows of ripening corn. Murderous rifle and artillery fire mowed everything down. The line of battle swept back and forth across this field 15 times. All that remained to be seen were rows of bodies.

Tah wrote a round robin letter to all members of our family from Hagerstown, Maryland. It pretty well gives the context of some of our brushes with history...

Dear Family:

In another letter, I told you it took us nearly all day to do the second day's five-mile-hike, remember? The very next day we had planned another five-mile-hike, were on the Trail at 8 a.m. and finished by *10:30 a.m.*! Boy, were we surprised! We were not even ready for lunch and we were through!! The difference was, of course, in the terrain. The previous day we were laden with our backpacks and had *very* steep grades to climb up and down with very bad footing. The following day was walking thru the woods on logging roads, flat and easy, not much elevation change and it was a boulevard!!

It was different today. We walked twelve miles—total time was seven and one-half hours including a whole one-hour lunch pause. So you see, time and distance varies. We try to keep our hiking under eight hours a day (preferably six) and regulate the mileage according to the difficulty of footing and the total number of mountains to be climbed.

Let me describe a typical day. As in September it still gets to be about 92-94 °F at mid-afternoon, we arise very early and hike in the cool part of the day. We have found it more and more difficult to locate restaurants in which we can have breakfast before 6 a.m.; therefore, we have cold cereal and fruit and bread and butter and coffee in our room after arising at *5 a.m.*! Yes, 5 a.m.! We leave by 6 a.m. in two cars which we brought on this trip. We leave one car at our exit point and drive the other to our entry point which Jim has figured out ahead of time. So we usually start hiking at 7 a.m. and by 11 a.m. we have our lunch-stop. Between 2 and 3:30 p.m. we have arrived at our car. Then we collect the other car and frequently then we

154

"go exploring" the countryside, assessing the village, the people, the social strata, the type, etc., as well as any historic significance or interest. Yesterday, we got steeped in Civil War history; saw the Museum and the historic site at *Antietam,* where one of the most important battles of the Civil War was fought. We got the whole background leading up to the battle and its significances as well. After a shower and swim, we seek a good restaurant in the area. Believe you me, there is quite an interesting variety; and by 9:30 we are sound asleep. We are up again at 5 a.m.; this schedule is for our "day hiking." The backpacking naturally is quite different. We try to schedule it so that we can reach the shelter by 3 p.m., find our water (!), and set up camp. As it gets dark by 8 p.m., we have to have eaten, cleaned up, strung up our food in a tree and be in our bedding by dark. We each carry a tiny flashlight; get up again as day breaks and we break camp right after breakfast and hike again until 3 p.m.

So you see, we are not "wearing any hair shirts"; we are enjoying the hiking as well as the exploring.

We are well aware that the hiking in Maine will be *much* more strenuous than here; so we are hardening ourselves and getting stronger daily. Pretty soon we'll be steel and skin (ha! ha!). On Tuesday we will be at Karen's for two days; Dad will be in N.Y.C. for Indian Head and then we go to Maine to be with Bob and Lucy et al. So we will have fun visiting, and a whole week of rest from hiking, after hiking ten days in a row.

Love,

XEF

Dear Family:

Were you aware that Benedict Arnold under George Washington led a troop of 1,100 men through the Maine Lake country (from N.Y. to Quebec) to attack Montreal? All but 600 men died or deserted. Needless to say, the attack failed. However, the Arnold Trail is part of the AT in spots. Now, where the poor men had to portage and carry the gear in the deep, ghastly winter, a lot of the places have "carry" incorporated in the name, such as, East Carry Pond, West Carry Pond, etc. They went up the Kennebec

155

River in boats and then west to Quebec, using the network of lakes to carry their equipment.

Pierce Pond Lean-to was on one of these lakes. In it was an ad posted for meals at a renovated fishing camp, breakfast for $2.25 with all the pancakes you can eat. As it was only one-quarter mile from the lean-to where we had arrived by four p.m., Dad and I went there for dinner. It was fantastic, especially in comparison to the meal we had planned for the night at the lean-to, noodles with dried chicken gravy. It was this renovated fishing and hunting camp, called the "Carrying Place," that we had heard so much about on the Trail. There is a regular "hot-line" on the Trail. Normally, one meets hikers in the lean-tos, or on the Trail, who provide the "latest dope" about the trail condition ahead, the sources of drinking water, the condition of the next lean-to and any other gossip of the Trail, such as, who the latest champion pancake eater at the Carrying Place is and how many pancakes he consumed. When we arrived there, forty-nine pancakes (dollar size) claimed the championship.

A couple, Dory and Bud Williams, who had just retired from Pennsylvania, had bought the run-down fishing and hunting camp, consisting of a large main building with a nice lounge and dining room and kitchen, surrounded by eight or so cabins. They had worked like beavers to recondition it so that it was habitable and were then trying to make it a "going proposition." Fishermen and hunters by the week are the most likely customers, plus hikers of AT, if they have the money. Deep in the wilds of Maine, it nevertheless is also accessible by an old logging road by car, so that townspeople occasionally also come, as the reputation of the food is growing. I wish them luck. They are a nice couple. Bud said that starting in mid-November they have over eight feet of snow until mid-April. They are also hoping that cross-country skiers will "find them."

Love,

KEF

156

Bud and Dory Williams introduce Tah and Jim to The Carrying Place.

Here lived a man of history

Monticello, the home of Thomas Jefferson, third president of the United States, is near Charlottesville, Virginia, less than a half hour's drive from the Appalachian Trail. Jefferson, in his epitaph, wanted to be remembered as "the author of the Declaration of American Independence, of the statute of Virginia for religious freedom, and father of the University of Virginia." He did not list the presidency as an accomplishment.

As a result of our visit to Monticello while we were hiking the Trail in the Shenandoah, I became more interested in Thomas Jefferson as a person. He is certainly among the most admired founding fathers because of his political service to his country, and because he was one of the most versatile and intelligent leaders in our early history. Along with Lincoln and the Bible, he is an oft-quoted authority on principles of democracy and decent public policy. Jefferson is on a pedestal and has always been a person of heroic proportions.

Knowing how great a historical figure he was, how liberal, intelligent and incisive he clearly must have been, I was disappointed to find that he said in his book, "Notes on Virginia," that he

believed that "blacks...are inferior to the whites in the endowments both of body and mind." This flaw in his character (in the sense that character is the total of physical, intellectual and spiritual qualities of a person as exhibited in thought and deed) raises a question of the credibility of his other lofty positions. I wonder how he could have so thoroughly endorsed our basic constitution. No matter that he is reported to have been completely opposed to the institution of slavery, he did own slaves like other southern gentility. Question: Would Thomas Jefferson have endorsed Aryan superiority or white supremacy over reds, yellows, and blacks? I believe that if he had been forced to make a hard decision, he would have come down on the side of the question with Lincoln and the Supreme Court of the United States.

Virginia seems to have an unusually large number of colleges and universities located near the Appalachian Trail. In addition to the University of Virginia, there are several familiar names of colleges along Interstate 81, paralleling the AT: Sweet Briar College, Mary Baldwin College, Washington and Lee University, Virginia Military Institute, and Emory and Henry College. We felt free to wander around these campuses during our leisure time, and we often did just that.

POSTED
PLEASE KEEP OUT
McAFEE'S KNOB,
This Fire Road and all Adjoining
Lands are privately owned
AND CLOSED
to the Public.
No Hiking - No Motorcycles
Please Keep Out - Posted

Signed: Property Owners; Catawba Mountain

In this quiet countryside, there are rumblings

The sections between Pearisburgh and Roanoke, Virginia, were memorable because of the tug-of-war raging between hikers and land owners in the Sinking Creek and the Catawba areas. Land owners had become so upset with hikers that in those two locations, involving some forty to fifty miles of trail, they had closed their land to hikers, posted the land, and requested the sheriffs to arrest and prosecute violators. And we heard that some hikers who got lost or who deliberately ignored the posted signs were arrested and fined. The probability is that the land owners were justifiably reacting harshly towards abuses against their property. Further, it is probable that week-end hikers, and not through-hikers, were the guilty ones. Those familiar with the through-hikers know that with practically no exceptions they are dedicated to avoiding and preventing abuses of any kind on the Trail or on adjacent properties.

Tah was grounded with a sore foot and therefore could not hike with me for a few days between Pearisburg and Route 311 at Catawba. So I tackled it alone with her support in shuttling. The prominent memories I have are the hikes on both sides of Newport, Virginia. I drove from Newport southwest on Route 601 to the point where the Trail crossed the road. The plan was that I would hike north on the Trail the estimated seven miles to Newport where Tah would meet me at twelve noon. As it turned out I limped into Newport at one-thirty p.m. where Tah had been patiently waiting for an hour and a half figuratively tapping her foot and wondering what happened.

I tried to explain. At the end of the first hour, I had coasted into the Big Pond Shelter, about two miles from where I had started at daybreak. Just before arriving at the shelter I had read a sign which said, "The next thirty-eight miles of the AT is a relocation; see details in Shelter." So, in the Shelter I carefully read the six handwritten pages pegged on the bulletin board, the first paragraph of which said that the next six miles are really tough. I said, "pooh" and by seven-thirty set out to continue my hike. Everything went smoothly, a pleasant day. I was alone with an occasional lone towhee. The air was clean and cool.

Then at nine-fifteen I stopped for a snack and a rest. I figured that I was within an hour and a half of completing the day's hike. What in the world would I do if I arrived at eleven o'clock, an hour ahead of schedule? Furthermore, I had not even worked up a sweat on this late August day. And the rest of the way was most likely downhill. Tah would not believe I had hiked if I weren't sweating! So I napped until ten o'clock. Then within five minutes after I started walking again, the trouble began. "The Trail is really tough" echoed from the bulletin board. I struggled and struggled, up and down and sideways for the next three and a half hours! I felt deceived; it was not seven miles; it was not eight miles. It seemed like ten or eleven miles of ungraded, rough, unworked trail, criss-crossed with blow-downs. Even the open meadow through which it eventually went for a short distance was too steep even for an Austrian hay farmer to work. And, of course, the day warmed up considerably by noon; it must have reached ninety degrees. By the time I got off the mountain, crossed the covered bridge and hiked the half mile to Route 42, I was in a sweating stew and practically lame. I was happy to see Tah.

Later in the afternoon at the motel in Blacksburg, severe cramps overtook both my legs. A quinine pill, a couple of bananas, a big dinner and a good night's rest restored my energy for the next day.

The relocations in the Sinking Creek and Trout Creek sections between Newport and Catawba were shunned by most who read the warnings at shelters along the Trail. The few who tried the new, relocated Trail in these sections in 1977 and 1978 told tales of excruciating hardships, involving scratches and lacerations from climbing over blow-downs, losing the way and re-hiking the already hiked section in the wrong direction, or getting confused with the old trail markers and being confronted with an irate land owner with shotgun.

At Catawba, the Trail was interrupted in the spring of 1978 and relocated off Catawba Mountain on to North Mountain because land owners became fed up with abuses on McAfee's Knob. This twenty-mile relocation was accomplished by the Roanoke Appalachian Trail Club in one week-end, after land-owners closed the original route.

Fortunately, there was a trail in place on the ridge of North Mountain which was a very pleasant walk for Tah and me. The greatest difficulty was in getting across from Tinker to North Mountain, which involved a sharp descent followed by a rugged crossing of pastureland and then a sharp ascent to the Trail again. All in all, we figured that we must have hiked an extra five or six miles as a result of this relocation.

A postscript to this story: As of November, 1980, the National Park Service and the Appalachian Trail community had substantially completed acquisition work to relocate the Trail through Catawba Mountain and over McAfee Knob. It was felt that the former route was so superior to the North Mountain route that the additional acquisition costs were justified.

For the record

Randy Gifford was having lunch at Fullhardt Knob Shelter. He was a rising junior at the University of Connecticut and he had to finish the Trail by Labor Day or shortly thereafter to return to college. We got to talking about Warren Doyle, who set the record of 66½ days for hiking the full length of the Appalachian Trail in one gulp. Subsequently, he had organized groups of fifteen to twenty University of Connecticut students to hike the Trail from

Springer to Katahdin in 1975 and following years. He was measuring their attitudes with psychological tests before and after. Out of this would come a PhD thesis. Randy also knew the student hikers and he marveled with me that only two out of fifteen failed to finish the Trail the prior year.

The word (probably apocryphal) on the "hot-line" on the AT was that a message was sent out from Harpers Ferry to Warren Doyle requesting that he treat the Trail for what it is, a walking path, not a race-track. Benton MacKaye's letter of March 1, 1972 (published in Edward B. Garvey's book, APPALACHIAN HIKER II) states: "...the A.T.—a pathway into the study of nature." On another occasion he also said that the Trail's purpose is "To walk. To see. And to see what you see."

Warren Doyle, by hiking the Trail in 66½ days, averaging 30.6 miles per day, recognized that he was not in tune with Benton MacKaye's stated purposes. He makes a statement in AP-PALACHIAN ODYSSEY by Steve Sherman and Julie Older: "I cried out of loneliness and from the pressures of the 'time-table'...beauty was everywhere but not the time to drink." (page 230) Warren is correct to maintain that nature can help one to satisfy a variety of needs, among them achievement and "character-confirmation," the purposes he sought to fulfill.

In the October 1, 1978 issue of The Roanoke Times and World News was a report that in 1978 "marathon runner, John Avery, 29, broke the speed record by going from Springer Mountain to Katahdin summit in 65 days 21 hours and 15 minutes." As the saying goes: records are made to be broken! (It should be noted that ATC does not record times; nor does it record the ages of "2000-Milers," preferring instead to promote Trail-founder Benton MacKaye's philosophy.)

On the inside wall of this covered bridge near Newport, Virginia, are two notices, or pleas, by the New York State Covered Bridge Society and by the Connecticut River Valley Covered Bridge Society of Greenfield, Massachusetts. Their plea was to "help preserve our remaining covered bridges." The following quotation supported the pleas:
"Remove not the ancient landmark which thy fathers have set."
Proverbs 22:28

Discretion is the better part of valor

We scratched and clawed our way up the mountain—but had to admit that Wildcat had won the day. We made a strategic withdrawal by way of gondola, with a vow to return to fight another day.

Dear Family:

We are nearing the end of our adventure; so now to the story of the finale, the final "turn of the screw" the Trail gave us, to command our respect for it, especially in New England.

September 12: We arrived at Pinkham Notch late evening. The night was bitter cold, a sample of what was to come; and, as it had been 94° in the shade when we packed to leave Tryon, I had not brought my down jacket.

September 13: Spent a good part of the a.m. shopping for a jacket for Tah and a small stove for backpacking, necessary in rain when wood is wet. Our little Gerry gas stove had quit working. After finishing shopping, we finally got started on the task of climbing Wildcat Mt. for overnight at Carter Notch Hut. (No service there.) Immediately got lost on a skiing trail and flailed about for almost an hour before returning to Pinkham Notch for more explicit directions as to where the AT was. Do you kids remember Wildcat? It wasn't too terrific a mountain, just looking at it straight on, was it? Our whole day's hike was less than seven miles...seems reasonable to make it before 6 p.m. (dark) even after a false start, now doesn't it? Well, it took us, loaded to the gills, from 1 p.m. to 4:45 p.m. to claw our way up a steep and rough path and cover exactly 2.7 miles. We were exhausted when we reached the top of Wildcat; and devastated when we realized we had gone 2.7 miles in almost 4 hours with 3.5 miles yet to go. Luckily, the ski gondola was still running at top; it took us exactly one second to decide on an "organized retreat" down the mountain in the gondola and to the lodge at Pinkham Notch.

September 14: This time we took the gondola up Wildcat and started where we left off yesterday to go to the shelter; got there by 3 p.m. Good thing we did our "one-day-hike" in two days; got to hut to find it officially closed but were allowed to sleep in a cabin; had our own food.

September 15: Carter Notch Hut to Imp Shelter, mainly in the rain. Only 7 miles but this also took all day, from 8 a.m. on as Trail was so steep. I had to *back down* the whole North Carter Mt. for one hour steady...most of the rest of the Trail I could handle going frontwards!!

We arrived at the Imp Shelter at mid-afternoon after a wet trip across from Carter Notch Hut. Rain had started at

7 o'clock that morning as we were getting ready to leave. We waited around for the weather report which is relayed to the huts by short wave radio at 8 a.m. daily from Pinkham Notch. The forecast was for rain ending around noon and then clearing. We took off and by noon the rain really did stop, but underfoot remained wet the rest of the way.

Imp Shelter was completely enclosed, more like a hut than a shelter. Three young men were already there and they cleared one-half of the floor space for our use. Bryan, Walter and Jim had finished a summer of camp counseling and were out for a couple of weeks of fun hiking and camping. From Imp they planned to go to the Presidentials, but they were in no hurry. They had brought along $75 worth of freeze-dried foods, bought at wholesale through their summer boss who owned a food company. As we arrived they were engrossed in making a reflector oven in which they could bake bread. The product was terrific.

September 16: On the way down from Imp Shelter to Route 2 at Shelburne, N.H. we had a visit with a schoolmaster and two students from the South Yarmouth School. They were the remnants of a school hiking club. We met them as they were climbing up the ridge about half-way to Imp where they planned to turn around. The boys said that the climax of the day's outing was going to be the stop for a fill of hamburgers and milkshakes at McDonalds.

September 17: Day of rest. I spent it in bed at the motel getting rid of a nasty cold. By next day I was up and rarin' to go.

John Sullivan is the owner of Shelburne Birches Motor Inn in Shelburne, New Hampshire, on Route 2—a short distance from the Trail crossing. He was from Boston and was married to a British nurse, whom he met when she came to Boston with a medical group. John was most generous to shuttle us and/or our car on two occasions, once to Pinkham Notch and again to Grafton Notch in Maine. He and Mrs. Sullivan miss Boston very much and it would not be surprising if they gave up their motel venture to return to the city.

Love,

KEF

The Trail is a majestic song—Of discoveries of self in the natural world

The rain
in Maine

The rain didn't stay mainly in the plain. It was everywhere and almost incessant. During one twenty-eight day stretch while we were in Maine it rained twenty-four days. Nevertheless, we feel that Maine provided the most exciting, the most challenging, and the most rewarding experiences on the Appalachian Trail. In addition to the challenges which we faced on Lower Jo-Mary Lake and in Mahoosuc Notch, we found ourselves deeply involved in wilderness which we had not known existed. We discovered things about ourselves which came forth only in Maine's natural setting.

Tah's letters capture and convey the delights we shared.

Dear Family:

We "have taken residence" in Maine these past four weeks and we have learned to love it. It is a lovely, wild, unspoiled state. Unfortunately, this fall the weather has been exceptionally wet. There was a bad drought until July; apparently the whole state was brown until then. And then the rains came and have not let up since. And it is COLD to boot. However, the fall foliage is fantastically beautiful. Somehow, the grey in the sky makes the yellows and the oranges sing even more. The rivers are swollen and the bogs are deep; even the Trail has rivulets flowing down it. And still we happily trudge through the mud and water.

Our four-day backpack of last week involved some unusual hiking experiences, such as fording three swollen

rivers by taking off our boots and pants and wading across
the cold and swift waters with our backpacks on our backs
and rainjackets on. We had a long pole in each hand to
steady ourselves, Jim leading and me whimpering behind
him, that is, on the second and third streams. In the first
stream, Jim forged ahead into that wild stream while I
watched with two native Maineites, Bud Ragan and Al
Papineau. After Jim got across, the men rock-hopped into
the middle of the stream and threw my boots and backpack
to Jim on the other side. I, bleating like a lost lamb and
thoroughly frightened at the whole thing, kept saying, "This
is nonsense. I'll take the gondola up the mountain
(Sugarloaf)." However, since my boots as well as my husband, in order of importance, were on the other side of
that wild, raging stream and I had three men to "talk me"
over, I finally, tremblingly, managed it.

The very next day there were two more such rivers to
cross; the bridge across one had been washed out. No more
bleating from me! I took off my boots and trousers; put on
my rainjacket (yes, it was pouring); took two long poles
and waded up to my thighs after Jim, without a murmur.
P.S. The water was darn cold!

The peaks we crossed were mostly in fog and drizzle;
but on the three-mile stretch above timberline on the ridge,
we were fortunate enough to have blue sky for thirty
minutes before the rain started in again. The nights in the
lean-tos were chilly and damp; yet the whole experience is
exhilarating and a lot of fun.

We "day-hike" where possible and then stay in motels.
But there is a lot of mileage that has to be done in
backpack trips. Carrying all that extra weight, up those
steep grades and then down again, really tests our mettle.
But the resulting views, if only a glance at a time and the
sense of accomplishment and of vigor are more than worth
it.

Let me quote you from the guide book* about the section we have just completed:

"This 30-mile section is the most difficult along the
AT in Maine. It crosses four 4,000 ft. peaks, passes close to

*Guide to the Appalachian Trail in Maine, ATC Publication No. 4, Eighth
Edition, 1975, Sec. 13, p. 183.

another and crosses three other peaks of about 3,000 ft. In addition, it has substantial gains and losses in elevation between these peaks. The net elevation gain is a substantial 10,100 ft. These represent the greatest net climb north of the Presidentials in N.H.

"Hikers should not underestimate the effort and time needed for the complete traverse of this section. Also, the hiker should be aware of the three-mile above tree-line traverse of the Horn and Saddleback Mountains. In inclement weather, this section can be dangerous. For the hiker, this is the most outstanding section of the western Maine mountains. Its high peaks and above tree-line climbing, its deep valleys, its mountain ponds and rock-strewn streams, all in a sublime wilderness setting, offer the best of Maine."

(P.S. And don't forget those endless soggy bogs-HF). Does this description give you an idea as to why we are enjoying it?

Love,

KEF

Bud Ragan talked Tah across a raging stream near Carrabassett.

During welcome moments of sunshine we dried out our most important equipment.

We could not have continued without Bud Ragan and Al Papineau. We found Bud managing the Shell service station at the junction of Highway 27 and the road leading up to Sugarloaf Ski area in Carrabassett Valley. We asked him if he knew anyone with a four-wheel drive who would drive us up the Caribou Valley Road to the intersection of the AT to let us out to day-hike back across North and South peaks of Crocker Mountain to Route 27. We had heard that the logging road had several bad washouts. We would like also to be driven in a second day to permit us to start a three-day backpack trip in the other direction across Sugarloaf, Spaulding and the Saddleback Mountains.

Bud immediately recommended that I get in touch with Al Papineau. Al was familiar with the road and readily agreed to take us in his Dodge four-wheel drive, eight gears, slant-6 engine, Ram Charger. It was an astonishing performance! He never had to use more than six gears but there were times when the Ram Charger was practically standing on its nose as it entered deep washouts which had become swollen mountain streams. Al nursed it through and up the steep inclines on the other side.

The next day Bud Ragan volunteered to come with us, I think because the gauge at the bridge showed the river we had to wade had risen several feet as a result of the heavy rains during the last twenty-four hours. As it turned out Bud was of inestimable value in teaming with Al to encourage and assist us in crossing the swollen stream.

Bingham, Maine

Dear Family:

Here we are in Bingham, Maine, a small hamlet, about 40 miles southwest of Monson. The roads are few, mostly going north and south. It is getting cool here. In the 30's at night and we are grateful for the down jackets and sleeping bags. We are re-learning that backpacking is a totally "different game" from just plain "day hiking." The last mountain we climbed (backpacking) was quite rugged, steep and rocky. At places we crawled on hands and knees; at other places I could put one foot up on a rock, but did not have the strength to pull up and straighten the leg with the added twenty-five pounds on my back. That trip was particularly slow because we were in rain for two days; the rocks were extremely slippery and the roots and moss over the rocks were even more slippery. It took us seven hours to do eight miles with only a brief stop for a Granola bar to eat. It is not conducive for a nice, long, restful lunch when it is cold and raining and there is a half-inch of water in the boots. When we reached the lean-to, we heated up some water to make hot soup and changed into dry clothes. We crawled into the sleeping bags after hot noodles and cheese.

In the morning it was still raining; our hiking clothes were still wet but we put them on, saving the dry ones to change into when we arrived at the next lean-to. The mental fatigue of carefully watching each step to keep from falling on the slippery ground was more than the physical fatigue. But it is extremely exhilarating to have this challenge and we really are enjoying it. Most of the time it is lovely scenery and an extremely pleasant experience.

Love,

KEF

177

Planning the hike is part of the challenge

Carrabasset Valley, Maine

Dear Family:

We are here in the western part of Maine, having just "emerged" from a three-day backpack trip over the Bigelow Mt. Range. I never knew too much about the Maine mountains before this; but we are learning to have a great deal of respect for them. The White Mountains seem much less rugged than these mountains here. The terrain

178

here is much rougher underfoot. Spending the nights in
lean-tos or under a tarp in the woods (instead of in a hut as
in the White Mountains) definitely calls for more stamina
and fortitude; and the trails are in more primitive condition, that is, not as well-groomed.

The countryside is at its height of beauty just now.
The colors are the vivid reds, oranges, yellow, as only New

England has. It is also quite cold here. The socks I hung up in the lean-to to dry overnight had frost on them the next morning. Have you tried hiking in frozen socks?

We seem glued to the weather reports these days; they definitely take precedence over the news under these conditions. In unsettled weather conditions we plan the day-hikes, waiting for a three-day fair weather forecast before we go off on an extended backpack trip. Thursday evening, the forecast was for fair weather until Sunday p.m. Hurrah! We decided to tackle Bigelow Mountain Range, about which we had heard enough to have a real proper respect!

We left early Friday morning, going north to south, as there is no lean-to for the first night; there are two well-spaced lean-tos for the next two nights. However, this way we climbed up (fully loaded with heavy backpacks) some incredible boulders; it was rock-climbing, hampered by the backpack. The boulders were huge and went straight up; S and E, remember that Madison Gulf Trail up to Madison Hut? Well, this was similar; only the boulders were much larger, and the Trail up that wall was much longer, 2,000 feet in one mile to be exact. And it was a gorgeous day, and challenging and fun. We were exhausted but exhilarated when we arrived on top to continue three miles.

At the end of the first day we stopped by a stream, cooked our supper and stretched out under our tarp, to be wakened by the sounds of raindrops, which then degenerated into a steady drizzle for all of Saturday. What a dumb weather report that had been! We packed up our wet and soggy things, it was about 40° so we were NOT warm, and after some hard soul-searching, continued onward, onto the next peak of over 4,000 feet where there was a lean-to just under Avery Peak. The thought of having climbed those big boulders up Little Bigelow only to turn back and not complete that whole range of mountains was what pushed us on, that and the eternal optimism of fair weather the next cloud away. Just after we had finished our supper at the Avery Lean-to, which was very cold with a bitter wind blowing in the drizzle (over tree line), five young men from Bowdoin College showed up. They were trail-crewmen. Cold, wet and energetic, seven of us huddled overnight in a lean-to meant for six, very cozy, somewhat cramped but cheery.

They told us that the Trail up the next two peaks was steep, very steep and slippery, above tree line and windy.

We donned our raingear and wet clothes and started off. We got a break; the clouds lifted, it was a lovely day, we had gorgeous views; we saw Katahdin to the northeast. The Trail was not nearly as steep as the one two days ago. We arrived at the next lean-to for late lunch. Although the sun was out, it was still very cold and windy. So we decided to "hike like crazy" and get off the mountains by night fall; there were some clouds building up on the horizon.

It was a long but interesting hike down from 4,120 to 1,100 feet from two p.m. to five p.m. in six miles. The threat of darkness kept us going at a good pace. We reached our car with a great feeling of accomplishment. During the night the rain started again and it is coming down in sheets now. We feel so smug and snug in our nice warm, dry motel, looking out the window at the deluge outside.

We heard over the radio it is in the high 70's in the south. It is in the 30's to 40's here. The fall foliage here is over a month ahead of Tryon. The lady at the motel is kindly letting me use the office typewriter, explaining that it skips, and that it does, unexpectedly. But it certainly is better than writing you all in longhand. We called Karen last night; no news from anyone; so we gather all is well.

We have asked Jean Boutilier to cull our mail while we are gone. We telephone her once every ten days or so, and we call Karen every weekend. In case someone must contact us, Jean will call Karen in an emergency.

It is doubtful that I will be able to get my hands on another typewriter soon. Postcards and notes will follow this if that is the case. You all know we are having a wonderful time, doing what we have always wanted to do and really well while doing it. It is so wonderful to be outdoors, expecially in New England mountains, being challenged by nature, but not overdoing it. True, we cannot do physically as much as we could twenty years ago, but there still is plenty of vigor and fun left. Perhaps another way of saying it, is, we now know what our limitations are and recognize them, whereas twenty years ago, we simply would not have recognized them. So there!

Love,

XSF

N otes on hiking trip, Blanchard to Caratunk, Maine.

Travel day: We drove up to Bingham from Fortune's Rocks, Maine, where we had visited over the weekend with Ralph and Eleanor Cole (at their seashore place) and with Bob and Lucy Flack and our grandchildren, Betsy and Jesse. Stopped at L.L. Bean's at Freeport and bought rain covers for our backpacks to supplant plastic garbage bags. Stayed overnight at Bingham Motor Inn, fifteen miles south of Caratunk. Mrs. Later manages the Inn. When we failed to return after a few days out on a hike, she called the Ranger at Caratunk who told her not to worry as we would probably be O.K. and would pay for the night reserved. She was incensed at his response; she called only because she was concerned for our safety.

Caratunk is a key "care package" post office, and Mr. Mitchell is the hiker's friend.

Where but in Maine are days like this?

First day: We parked our Chevy across from the Ranger Station in Caratunk and drove around to Blanchard where we parked our Pinto in the driveway of Mrs. Ross with her permission. She was from Ohio, summering in her place in Maine. A clear, blue day 33°-60°; where but in Maine are days like this?! 10.4 mile day to Moxie Bald Lean-to.

Second day: Still 33°-60° *but* rain all day, at times heavy. "Where but in Maine?!" 5.1 miles to Joe's Hole Lean-to.

Third day: Continued rain. A steep and slippery climb up Pleasant Pond Mountain. 8 miles to lean-to.

Fourth day: Downhill all the way. Jeep trail and Pleasant Pond Stream to Kennebec River at Caratunk. Clear and blue again. 5.5 miles, out by 10:30 a.m. Tah and I bought knitted AT hats from woman in town. Also ordered some for grandchildren with names knitted in.

Best laid plans
can go astray

We started out at Monson on a clear day at the decent hour of nine in the morning. We had enough food in our backpacks to last ten days to hike the one hundred miles north to the Abol Bridge Store, the next and only place to get supplies going north in this section. According to our guide book there are lean-to shelters every eight to ten miles; so we had decided not to carry a tent which saved us six and a half pounds. Even so, Tah had thirty-five pounds on her back at the beginning and I had fifty pounds. Altogether we had forty pounds of food to average two pounds per day per person. We thought that we had very heavy packs until we met others who carried heavier loads. A big, six-foot five-inch kid from Colorado was lugging seventy pounds, including forty pounds of food plus winter clothing. He and his partner planned to hike the entire Trail to Georgia between Labor Day and January 15. To do this they were going to have to average sixteen miles a day, which is normal for twenty-year olds.

The Appalachian Trail in eastern Maine is quite different from segments in other states. There are three features which are different: 1) drinking water is plentiful, clear and healthful in most places; 2) the Maine bogs are something to behold and to hike; 3) there are no such things as "graded trails" in eastern Maine; nor are there any switch-backs in mountainous terrain. The Trail goes straight up to the top of the mountain and straight down the shortest way.

The drinking water at springs and lean-tos was good. After the first few days we had streams and springs all along the Trail, particularly in the flat country. We drank directly from streams, lakes and springs without fear of pollution or upset stomachs. In most other sections one has to be careful about water, to have enough and to avoid pollution.

Throughout this section the bogs were numerous and the Trail through them was in various degrees of maintenance, mainly poor. Most were just mud because of the relatively dry summer. In my first jolting exposure to the Maine bogs, I lost my shoe. I happened to have changed my boots to Wallabees as we were backtracking trying to find a shelter which our six-year old guide book said existed. My foot slipped off a split-log laid in a bog and I plunged into the mud. I pulled my foot clear but my shoe stayed stuck in the mud. To free the shoe I had to take off my backpack and pull the shoe out with both hands to break the suction.

The next experience I had was to slip off a log into slush. This time I sank in above my knee with one foot and leg. Fortunately, I had my heavy boots on and was able to maneuver my foot out intact after a short struggle.

The other experience we had with bogs brought on a crisis. Tah's foot slipped in a bog and she sprained her ankle. She then hobbled seven miles to a cabin where we had to hole up for a couple of days until she could walk again. We were still some thirty-five miles from Abol Bridge. As related in "Enough Wasn't Enough," we made it out under our own power after some tense waiting.

In some places the beavers had dammed up the bog streams and raised havoc with the Appalachian Trail. One time we faced the AT blaze on a tree which was in the middle of a pond with no way to walk to it. We had to back out and follow new blazes around to the left to bypass the beavers' work.

The Appalachian Trail in eastern Maine zigs and zags from mountain to mountain and lake to lake. This was particularly excruciating to us the first six days, between Monson and Whitecap Mountain Lean-to, a total of about forty-two miles. In this distance we ascended and descended six mountain peaks involving vertical changes each time from 1,000 feet to 2,000 feet. On the face of it, this does not sound too strenuous. However, with full packs on the back, and with no graded trail, these vertical ascents and descents were really demanding. They actually added a full day to our schedule and caused us to have to stretch our food at the end. The best we could average through these mountains was eight miles a day versus the ten a day planned.

Our guide book had not pointed out an exception to its statement that there were lean-tos every eight to ten miles in the eastern section of the AT in Maine. There was a seventeen-mile segment between Chairback Mountain Lean-to and Whitecap Mountain Lean-to with no shelter. The listed White Brook Lean-to had burned and the Trail had been relocated. But there was a campground at Gulf Hagas on the newly located route. As it turned out we slept under the stars by the Gulf Hagas Brook, the fifth night out, with no adverse consequences except our sleeping bags got wet from the dew. We had also slept out in the open the first night out, even though we had the choice of sleeping in the Stanchfield cabin. We did not find the cabin until after we were pretty well set up for the night two hundred yards upstream. The other experience of sleeping out in the open occurred the third night. Our plan had been to hike the ten miles from Long Pond Stream Lean-to to Chairback Gap Lean-to; but this was the section involving ascending and descending five peaks with no switchbacks. We became exhausted after ten hours and sought refuge at West Chairback Pond, one-quarter of a mile off the Trail, which reportedly had a lean-to. This was our thirty-fourth anniversary night! There was no lean-to. But there were several rowboats and canoes beached at a campsite. We decided to sleep in the open in the woods nearby, knowing that if it did start raining we could prop up a couple of the boats on their ends or sides to provide shelter for our sleeping bags. During the night it did start raining and we did have to use the boats for shelter. The next morning we hiked in a downpour the one and a half miles to the Chairback Gap Lean-to and holed up for the rest of the day while it rained heavily. Three young men had also holed up there for the day, two from Colorado and one from Vermont. All three of them planned to hike the Trail well into the winter months.

The lean-tos in Maine were built originally during the Depression in the 1930s by CCC crews. They are of native log construction with a metal roof, shaped somewhat like a New England salt-box house but with the front side open. The sleeping area accommodates six people and generally is covered with split-logs with the rounded side up. As Tah said, it was like sleeping on a roll-top desk and about as uncomfortable. We collected limbs from storm-felled fir or balsam trees to spread over the sleeping surface whenever we could. This softened the floor a bit and added a marvelous odor to the night.

The lean-tos were always located near water, usually a stream or a lake of lovely, clear water which we drank, cooked with, washed clothes in and bathed in. At night we had to suspend our backpacks and food from the ceiling and tightly cover the packs with plastic to try to keep out the mice. They were real pests. Some hikers made no attempt to keep them out of their packs; instead they set up a small store of food or nuts in a corner to keep the mice occupied and away from their packs.

In some sections of the Trail in eastern Maine the going was pretty hard because of the "blow-downs" which had not been cleared from the Trail. About ten months earlier, in November, 1974, a storm with up to 175 mile-per-hour winds had swept through Baxter State Park and other sections where the Trail ran. The result was devastating to the forests; acres of trees had been leveled like straws of wheat. There followed a long debate among rangers and conservationists over what to do about the fallen timber. Some argued that the forest would be better off letting the dead wood lie and rot to provide mulch for new growth. Others

The Maine lean-to floor is like
a roll-top desk.

argued for salvaging the timber and using the proceeds to replant the areas affected. The latter plan was finally adopted. (We heard that subsequently a conservation group challenged this decision and sued to have it overturned to force compliance with the terms of the will which donated the land to the state, to preserve the land forever in its natural state.) In Baxter State Park alone the estimate was to salvage some 50,000 cords of wood which would sell for four dollars a cord on site. In many places hikers have had to hike around or climb over these blow-downs which added many miles and hours to the trek between Monson and Katahdin.

Between the blow-downs and the huge boulders which Tah had to scramble over, her khaki trousers were torn to shreds in the seat. Cleverly she cut off the legs below the knees and patched the seat with the leg cloth and safety pins.

Dear Family:

Have any of you ever heard of a "truck rodeo?" While we were in Bingham, Maine, a small hamlet on the Kennebec River, having our breakfast in the one restaurant for miles around, we were treated with the sight of "the truck parade" on the way to the rodeo, two miles up the road. Some thirty to forty 18-wheel log trucks rumbled down the road at about fifteen miles per hour, all with their headlights on, while their friends and families lined the sidewalks, waving and shouting encouragement. We did not go to the rodeo, as we had a long hike planned that day; but we were told that it consists of all kinds of contests: parking those huge trucks in small places in an allotted time, loading up the trucks in the shortest time, running obstacle courses, etc. People from miles around came to root for their favorite truck-team. Prizes were plentiful.

In that section of Maine, logging is the mainstay of the economy. It is seasonal and fairly unskilled; it can be learned in two weeks and it's a high risk occupation. Floating or logdriving in the Kennebec River has been the means of transporting these logs after they were cut; for years this had been the case. Then, last year, at the behest of the environmentalists, a state senator got a bill passed prohibiting the use of the river for driving the logs. The river had become extremely dirty and sludgy from the resin and bark from all those pine trees. The river is now cleaning itself up. The logs are being transported by truck.

And the senator is thoroughly hated by the local inhabitants. For several generations, in the small communities on the Kennebec River, most of the men earned their livelihood as logdrivers on the river. Fathers taught sons, and now suddenly—inside a year—their livelihood is gone. "The senator took the bread from our mouths and the roofs from over our heads." Naturally, the truck drivers now have those jobs, but they are not the same men; the logdrivers are displaced men. They must go on unemployment or move away and find new skills.

We met the wife of one such man, a Vietnam veteran, who is now in a nine-month training school for masonry in northern Maine. His wife and handicapped child are at home in Caratunk, alone for nine months. She is knitting woolen hats to supplement their income while he is at school. This couple will adjust to the change as they are young and flexible. For the older men, the future is dim. But the river has cleansed itself; the fish are now thriving again. All change, even for the good, has its price.

Love,

KEF

Prizes and Price

This truck will likely enter a rodeo on a summer weekend.

Baldpate Mountain was icy on top...

On top of Old Bald Pate all covered with snow

Western Maine

Dear Family:

In an earlier letter I mentioned how we learned to cross the engorged brooks by taking off our boots and pants and wading across. At the end of a thirteen-mile, hard day-hike, when we knew that we would spend the night in a dry motel room, we finally ended up by rolling up our pants and wading through the river with our boots

on; they were so wet anyway it really no longer mattered. We also found ourselves, at the end of a hard hike, no longer trying to keep our boots dry above the laces in the boots. We simply clomped through the middle of all that gook, just as long as the mud did not go over the top of the boots. How one changes when one is tired!

Our hiking last week was confined mainly to day-hikes. It has gotten VERY cold. There was a killing frost the other night. The top of Bald Pate Mountain, height of 4,000 feet, had ice and frost on it two days ago. It makes crossing those huge granite slabs above timberline in a very cold and strong wind somewhat tricky, as you can imagine, tricky and miserably cold until you get out of the icy blast and onto rock that does not have that thin sheet of ice on it. The day we were up there, though, was one of the six

clear days we had in the last five weeks. And the view was *gorgeous* and worth every miserably cold, sloggy and icy minute we had getting up there. That day was unbelievably beautiful, with the blue sky, the difficult climb up to the rocks, the treacherous footing, the very steep descent followed by a lovely runout along a large brook with many gurgling waterfalls, climaxed by a deep gorge for the tumbling water. What a fantastic way to end a perfect day, footsore and weary though we were!

Love,

K&F

But Fryebrook Gorge was free-flowing. This was one of the finest hikes on the whole Trail.

195

A song goes on

The day broke cloudy and threatening. We were disappointed because we were afraid that the Ranger would not open Katahdin for hiking. We were psychologically hopped up and ready to go. So the waiting for the signal to go or not go was frustrating.

Finally, at nine o'clock, he posted the all-clear signal! We practically got off to a running start; we were so happy to get the chance to climb that mountain.

The weather was ominous; the wind was high and gusts were severe. But the rain held off. We had no problems following the Trail upstream to the first rock-climbs. We had expected these to be quite difficult; at least the grapevine said so. However, the grooming of the trail through the boulders was superb. A little care was necessary, but there was nothing severe to cope with.

The toughest part of the day was beyond Thoreau Spring, out in the open, above treeline. The gusting, howling wind, quartering on our left, made it very tricky to hold a steady course. It not only

KATAHDIN STREAM
ALL HIKERS MUST REGISTER ON PORCH.
COVERED TABLES IN CENTER RING ARE FOR
PICNICKING AND DAY USE ONLY.
FIRES ARE PERMITTED AT SITES WITH A
FIREPLACE.

RANGER STATION

OFFICE & HIKING
REGISTER ⟶
B&P.

required a great deal more energy to walk; but the wind also forced us to concentrate mightily on where to step.

After a couple of hours, we took a rest-break in a semi-sheltered nook. Down the Trail behind us, and coming on at a good pace, John Collins was gaining on us. Impulsively, I called to Tah, "Come on. Let's get going. I'll not have a sixty-two year old pass me on Katahdin!" She said, "Okay, but I must remind you that you also had your sixty-second birthday last month!" Chagrined, I could mumble only the cliche, "Age is an attitude, not a number."

We made it in good time to the top, registered that we were there and ate a small lunch. We were glad that the course did not require our crossing on The Knife Edge in that gusting wind.

Since no overnight camping was allowed on top, we had to return to the bottom. Although this climb of Katahdin was not the final hike completing the Trail for us, we got a small feel of the joy the through-hiker must embrace as he finishes there.

We Remember People

We especially remember Margaret Stevenson, formerly of our home town of Tryon, N.C. That's Margaret and Tah at left, making up for months of not having seen each other.

The Tryon Trail Trotters make an annual trip to Townsend, Tennessee, practically on the northwest border of the Great Smoky Mountains National Park. Their purpose is to hike various trails in the Smokies for a few days as a kind of climax to their twice-a-week hikes nearer home and in the Pisgah National Forest. We hiked off the AT to Cades Cove and joined the seventeen members for dinner at Wilson's Restaurant. To have dinner with our Tryon friends was a nice change from our usual routine. We spent the night in the Valley View Motel.

Among the seventeen friends at Wilson's Restaurant were Bill and Margaret Stevenson from Maryville, Tennessee. Bill had retired as minister of the Tryon Congregational Church. Margaret may have retired with Bill but her hiking miles and time increased greatly. She had hiked twenty-seven days out of the prior thirty! She's a strong, fast hiker—has hiked every trail in the Great Smokies. Margaret reports that the wild animals of the Smokies aren't nearly as pestiferous as the local dogs on the streets of Tryon where she used to ride her bicycle at six in the morning!

If anyone ever acted to "help a fellow creature on his path"—as the twin kings sang in *The Gondoliers*—it was Gil St. Thomas, gate keeper at Abol Bridge for Great Northern Paper Company. That's Gil, at his daily post, hearing Tah out as she recounts our fourteen days in the Maine wilderness. He invited us inside his gate-house, seated us comfortably, brewed a pot of coffee and said quietly, "We'll get you into Millinocket. Don't you worry." Before long he hailed a station wagon driven by Mrs. Nancy Pray, the wife of Congressman Pray. He introduced us and asked her to give us a lift. She did. God bless them both.

We were a diverse string of hikers in the Great Smoky Mountains National Park. We met Bob first at Mollie's Ridge Shelter and a few days later again between Ice Water Gap Shelter and Tri-Corner Knob. He was from Connecticut and he planned to go all the way, maybe. He had started once earlier that year but had quit. He had come back to try it again. Bob had recently completed his Master's degree in electrical engineering and he was not quite ready for a job. When we last saw him, he was "humping" it so that he could finish a twenty-mile day and the Park by nightfall.

A lso at Mollie's Ridge Shelter were Dave, who was a State Park
Ranger at St. Augustine, Florida, and a young architect from
Rochester, New York, who took a five-year course at Kent State.
The Ranger was on leave and the architect was between school and
a job. At the same shelter was a young redhead who was a
transplant from New York City. He lived in Cosby, Tennessee whence he commuted daily to his job in a livery stable in
Gatlinburg. Red was getting married in three weeks. His father
was planning to retire and come to North Carolina soon. "What
does his father like to do?" "Work!"

J eff was originally from Illinois but he had been lifeguarding
at Key Biscayne, Florida. He was the youngest of the crew at age
twenty-one. He had no particular plans for school or work after he
completed the AT. He was a bit fed up with the duties of a lifeguard. "It's a boring job." He would prefer teaching swimming.
He had rescued over a hundred people from drowning. "It's hard
to understand why people try to travel across deep, open water
towards land on the other side when they know they cannot
swim!" he declared. "Furthermore, very few are embarrassed by
or grateful for the rescue." Jeff said that a lifeguard is finely at-
tuned to unnatural situations and events. He spots them and helps if
needed.

A t Tri-Corner Shelter we met Andy and Becky, a very enjoyable
couple from St. Louis. She was going for her PhD in chem-
istry, while he was studying bio-medical engineering. That's obviously a narrow specialty, having to do with machines, gadgets,
tools and devices of useful application in the field of medicine.
Andy and Becky had driven in two days from St. Louis to the
Smokies to hike various trails but not the entire AT.

A t Cosby Knob Shelter, there were five of us: two Jeffs, one
Sandy and we two. One of the Jeffs was our friend, the ex-life-
guard from Key Biscayne. The other Jeff was a plastic surgeon
who had just finished interning at the University of Virginia. Tah
asked him why a thirty-year old plastic surgeon would be out there
on the Trail with the rest of us. He replied that he had been constantly in school for umpteen years and had had no adolescence

and no identity crisis. He had not had time for them. Now, he thought, would be a good time to have at least his identity crisis before starting his practice. He could not think of a better location for it than the Great Smokies!

His friend, Sandy, was from the state of Washington but living in Chicago where he represented shipping interests for the Port of Seattle. Their mothers were long-time friends, and the boys had grown up together. They had planned a long time for this trip on the AT.

We had asked one of the waitresses in a diner at Blairstown, N.J. if she knew anyone who would drive us to our entry point on the Appalachian Trail so that we could complete the last nine-mile segment in New Jersey. She turned to Jerry, a customer sitting at the counter, and asked him if he would. He readily agreed to do it as soon as he finished his Sunday morning breakfast.

Jerry told us that he was somewhat familiar with our state of North Carolina, having had Marine training at Cherry Point. Following that stint he had gone to Vietnam for thirteen months. After discharge he had returned to his native town of Blairstown and had taken a job with Hoffman-LaRoche, a drug manufacturer.

The prior year he had gone with his girl friend and her family to Alaska, driving a recreational vehicle there and back in one month's time. He shared the driving chores with his girl friend's father, averaging 700 to 800 miles each day for sixteen hours a day. Roads were fine until they got on the Alcan Highway. They hardly got to their destination when they had to turn around and start back. He would now like to fly to Alaska and spend some time there.

He said that most of the G.I.s in Vietnam knew that it was a foolish war, strictly run by politicians. They were frustrated by two things: the "no-win" policy and the stories of draft card burning and protests back home. He agreed that Frances Fitzgerald's conclusion in "Fire in the Lake" is correct, which is that the French and the Americans had interfered with a revolution which inevitably must be consumated in Vietnam. In her book she said that it had been going on for a hundred years and may continue for another century, but it will go on to a conclusion.

Vance Trull, above, head of the Print Shop at Fontana Village, drove us to our entry points south of Fontana Dam on two successive days. In addition to having steady employment in the village, he is a professional hunting and fishing guide on holidays and during vacations. And in the weekly off-hours, he is a "music maker"; he and a small group of cronies are available for hire to provide the music for dances or religious occasions in the area. How's that for versatility?

Tony owns his own taxi in Greenwood Lake, N.Y. "No Smoking" signs were prominently displayed inside his car. Tony described, in some disgust, his brother in Florida as one who smoked "one after another." He said, "I keep asking him why he smokes; what's he trying to get out of it!" He continued, "I don't even smoke, but I'll catch cancer from inhaling smoke from twenty-five others, and from different brands, all during the day." Tony was very unhappy.

A lso, in Greenwood Lake, on another day, we hired the County Wide Taxi, driven by a New York City bus driver, named John Mulchey (pictured above between Tah and me). A few weeks earlier he had a call from the New York City Police Department telling him there was an opening for him on the force. That was a job he had applied for four years earlier and had wanted very much. But when it came he turned it down, deciding to stay with the Transit Authority where he had a chance to go "inside" as a mechanic's helper.

John worked twelve hours a day, four hours overtime. "It's tough," he said, "but I'm looking forward to the 'inside' job. The way traffic is, drivers don't give you a break." However, he admitted that he preferred to drive a bus rather than a car in New York City.

K enny McNamara shuttled for us for two days. Mrs.Castellano, wife of one of the owners of a hardware store in Culver Lake, N.J., had telephoned Kenny for us.

Kenny is the oldest of nine children, four boys and five girls. The children ranged in age from twenty-six down to the mid-teens. The oldest girl, twenty-four, was married. All the rest were at home. Kenny was tall and overweight; but "the others are skinny," he said.

The boys all worked for father. Kenny called it jokingly

"slave labor." Kenny drove a truck. The father was a scaffolding contractor but he also bought houses and fixed them up to sell. Kenny said his father was not about to make him a partner.

"Fadder" liked cameras; he had a dozen. Kenny had a cheap Kodak which he bought in Miami three years earlier. "It's not wrecked yet."

Mother and Daddy McNamara never fought, but the kids did all the time. The mother was forty-nine and had her birthday shortly after Mother's Day. Kenny planned to give her a "Big Kiss" for Mother's Day.

Kenny drove us to High Point and returned our car to Worthington Bakery to park it. As agreed, he hid the key inside the fender over the left rear wheel. He mildly tried to refuse pay but accepted six dollars the first day and five dollars the second day. He's an excellent driver.

Ray's taxi which we hired on two consecutive days for hiking near Hanover, New Hampshire was an experience. Ray owned and drove his own taxi, working off the taxi stand in front of the Hanover Inn.

He actually lived in West Hartford, Vermont, as did his six children and their spouses. He owned and drove a tractor-truck for twenty-five years, hauling other people's trailers all over the country. He was gone weeks at a time, leaving his wife to handle the children. He finally gave that up and started the taxi business, about fifteen years earlier. "It's much easier," he says. One of his sons owned a farm, another worked for the state as a forest warden and the third for a contractor. Ray stopped at the farmer son's house to introduce his daughter-in-law and two grandchildren to us. When he asked his daughter-in-law to verify how many children he, Ray, had, she said, "Too many" and went on to discuss what was happening with her children.

Ray pointed out a delapidated old house next door to his son's house in which a hermit was living. "He's a tough old bird; hasn't taken a bath in fifteen years. But he's kind and gentle with the grandchildren."

We surmised that someone in Illinois has "turned on" the students about the Appalachian Trail. The prior spring in

Southern Virginia, we had met a botanist and five of his students from a Community College in Chicago on a study tour. Again, the following fall we ran into another student group of fifteen from Illinois on the AT for ten days. And again, a few weeks later we met Jeff from Illinois State who is majoring in ecology. Jeff will do a thesis on trail maintenance. I recommended to him that he study how it's done not only in Jefferson National Forest, but also in the Shenandoah and the White Mountains of New Hampshire.

This is similar to the advice I gave to a member of Congress from our district in North Carolina when he sent us a questionnaire asking his constituents to state what advice they had if the Federal Government funded a project to acquire a large tract of land for recreational purposes. I urged him to insist on getting the expertise of the Appalachian Mountain Club and the Appalachian Trail Conference.

We picked up a young hitchhiker wearing a backpack as we came out on the highway above James River, after completing the dramatic ten miles over Bluff Mountain. His name was also Jeff and he was from Wisconsin. He was hitching north and around the next section to get into the Shenandoah. He had started in Georgia in mid-March, intending to go to Katahdin. An ice and snow storm in Georgia caused his seventeen-year-old brother to slip and badly hurt his leg. Jeff helped him to get home by bus. They did not have enough money to hire medical services in Georgia or North Carolina but did have bus fare. They had hobbled out at Deep Gap, N.C.

Near James River we met Joe Metz from Detroit Edison. He came to hike the AT for two to three weeks every annual vacation. He was about to complete 900 miles that day. His wife, Dorothy, would not accompany him, even though he offered to carry all the gear. We found that spouses often have split opinions on this subject.

Since we were in Georgia in late April and early May, we ran into very few people planning to go to Katahdin. We checked the Trail register on top of Springer and estimated that some 425 had registered in late March and early April, many of them intending to go all the way. So we felt that the first wave had already cleared Georgia. We did meet a few residents of Georgia who were out for two or three days, like the Bethels, a husband, "Butch," and his wife who were a pharmacist and a librarian from Griffin.

On top of Standing Indian (5,498 feet), appropriately called "The Grandstand of The Southern Appalachians," we met two couples enjoying the sun and a lunch break. The couple from Connecticut had only until mid-May to hike because they had jobs awaiting them. They planned to hike the trail over a period of years during vacations. The others were Dave and Debbie. Dave wore a baseball cap with a "P" on it, which stood for the first letter of a town in New York where he played summer baseball. I guessed wrongly that the reason he was headed for Wyoming at the end of August was to take a job after having finished a business school like Harvard, Wharton, or Tuck. Actually, he was going there to continue studying English in the Graduate School of the University. He had received an appointment as a teaching assistant.

Our hearts went out to the young doctor and his girl friend, a recent graduate of a nursing school. They had been on the Trail three days and nights and were on the verge of chucking the whole idea. He had just completed his medical training and was about ready to set up a practice somewhere. But before doing that he had the tremendous urge to hike the Appalachian Trail. He had gone on short hikes before but never anything like this. She had never gone hiking anywhere before and she did not like this one bit. She said that she was a city girl. They had started out at Katahdin with new, unbroken-in boots. Their feet were "blossoms of white," covered with moleskin and adhesive tape to ease the pain of blisters. They had no sneakers or loafers or wallabees into which to change in camp at night; so they limped around in their boots while they fixed supper. He had carried her pack on his stomach the last mile as they both limped into the Rainbow Stream Lean-to the night we met them. She was in misery. He talked of continuing, at least to Monson, eighty-five miles away. She talked longingly of turning back and getting home to New Orleans.

The following day, Tah in a burst of sympathy donated her

sneakers to the girl. Since they had already gone, Tah asked the next south-bound hiker to carry the sneakers to the nurse. We were quite sure that the young man could overtake the doctor and nurse

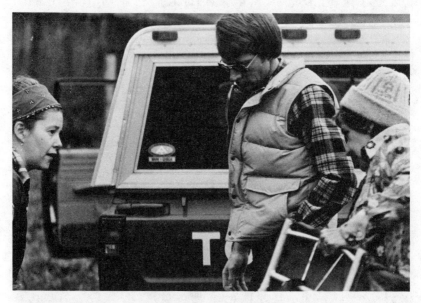

Tah likes the light and sturdy bamboo poles Bruce gave us.

soon. But we guessed that chances were even that he would meet them rather than overtake them.

On a hike from Wesser to Tellico Gap we met Bruce and Polly Hogshead from Berryville, Virginia, where Bruce was Division Materials Manager for Boise Cascade. Like us, they were hiking the AT during vacations and on weekends over several years. Unlike us, however, they were backpacking the whole Trail. On the day we met, they planned to spend the night in their tent on top of Wayah Bald; we planned to sleep in a motel room at Wesser. We made a date to meet them at Wayah Gap the following morning to drive them to Franklin, N.C. They had previously mailed to themselves a "care package" of food and clean clothing and they wanted to pick it up before the Post Office closed for the weekend. The Post Office was closed when we arrived, but the Postmaster was in and responded to Bruce's plea for the package.

We have enjoyed seeing the Hogsheads on other occasions when we hiked through their country in Northern Virginia. Once, early in the morning on his way to work, Bruce drove to an intersection of the Trail and a highway near Berryville, Virginia planning to leave two bamboo walking staffs for us, with a note attached. We were already there and ready to start when he arrived. We were delighted to have the bamboo staffs, cut from their own property, and we finished the rest of the Trail, 900 miles, with them. Tah found the use of a staff or pole indispensable. It provided the means of maintaining balance on logs or crossing creeks.

We were interested in how the Hogsheads got started on the Trail. Bruce first got the urge to hike the whole AT and became determined to do it during vacations. He had a problem. His wife showed dissidence by her silence. Bruce very much wanted her to hike the Trail with him. But like Brer Fox, she "lay low." Bruce bought books and maps and backpack. He spent evenings studying. Polly showed signs of real concern when, after three months, Bruce came home with a tent, a sleeping bag and dried foods. On the weekend he loaded his pack, put on his newly bought boots and took off for a nearby mountain to start training. Polly began to realize that "lying low" was not the correct strategy if she wanted to be with Bruce during vacations. By the time he got his boots broken in, she asked whether she could join him. Together they got Polly outfitted, broken in and indoctrinated into hiking and backpacking.

When we met them, it was hard to tell which was more enthusiastic, Bruce or Polly. They seemed to be equally involved in planning and working towards completing the Trail. Bruce worked normal holidays so that they could lengthen vacations to hike.

We came to know Harold Hoffman in Cosby, Tennessee when we were staying at the Laurel Springs Motel, which was in easy reach of Davenport Gap in the Great Smokies. Mrs. Nina Valentine, who with her husband owned the motel, called Mr. Hoffman and asked him to shuttle us around. When we first met him, he and his wife were living in a mobile home, their retirement home. The Hoffmans had vacationed in Cosby six years before deciding to make their home there. He had been an inspector in a laboratory serving Boeing Company, the airplane manufacturer.

His job was in quality control. He had lived most of his working life in Toledo, Ohio and Petersburg, Michigan.

When we saw him the second time, three years after having first met him, he told us that his wife had died a few months earlier. He said, "After she died, I was sitting in the trailer, alone. I decided that I would buy a pack of cigarettes or a fifth of Old Granddad. I decided on the cigarettes because I knew what would happen if I took another drink."

Mr. Hoffman said that he used to be a hard drinker, often downing a full bottle before noon. But it never showed. At night when he was at a bar, when it was time to go home, he would call a taxi and two drivers, one of them to drive his car home. He said that he never drove when drunk. One day in the middle of a drinking bout at his daughter's house, he quit. He got up and walked out. She called him to take his half-empty bottle. He said, "No. I'm through! I'll never drink again." She saved the bottle for him. He never picked it up.

Between Damascus and Pearisburg in late May and early June we met many through-hikers. Several times we met Phillip Hodges and John Lumsden, recent high school graduates of Clarkesville, Georgia. With them were Joy Edmondson of Santa Rosa, California and Ronald Betts of Hampton, New Hampshire, a couple of years older but obviously in tune with Phil and John. We met them four days in a row as they were hiking north and we were leapfrogging our two cars south to north but hiking south each day. The astonished look on their faces as we met and they recognized us on the second day was a rare sight to behold! The following days we looked forward to our short but cheerful reunion of "old friends" daily. Late one afternoon we picked up the foursome as they were hitchhiking from Groseclose to Marion to get a good meal; the local restaurant was closed for repairs. The following day, when we met them on the Trail again, we surprised them with two bottles of wine to celebrate their completion of 500 miles or one-fourth of the Trail. Their note on our windshield, thanking us for our friendship, warmed our hearts.

Also, in this southwest Virginia section was a young law student who said that he had been lost for three days, wandering from

213

one trail to another. At last he had found his way and was headed back to his car to return to Baltimore. He said that he had not begun to specialize in his study of law, but he knew that some day he would be on the Supreme Court!

The last tower we visited on the Trail was on Killington Peak in Vermont, in October, 1977. We had paused for a rest and to enjoy the grand view when from the tower above rang out a friendly, female voice, "Come on up for a visit." We climbed up, and had a delightful session with a mid-twentyish woman and her male companion who was keeping her company on a gray day.

She avowed that it had not been too difficult to qualify for the lonely job. It was just the kind of thing she wanted to do—not too strenuous but quite responsible. She invited us to look in upon her living quarters below. The "apartment," built among the footings at the base of the tower, was very attractive. There was electricity, but no running water that we saw.

We imagined that November would be the loneliest month, in between the seasons for hiking and skiing. Not far from the tower at the top of the ski lift was the "warming hut." But in all likelihood there was no need to tend the tower once ski season began.

The numbers of fire or lookout towers in the national forests are on the decline. The Appalachian Trail is often routed along ridges or across peaks, which command wide sweeps of the surrounding forests. Naturally the Trail guide books refer to the towers as Trail guideposts. More and more we came upon concrete footings where towers had been but had been dismantled. We wondered what was happening. The response to our inquiry was that the helicopter patrol is a lot more efficient and less costly.

Occasionally, kitchen help at our motel or inn drove us to our entry point in our car and brought the car back. Steve was the chef at "The Inn at Long Trail" at Sherburne Pass, Killington, Vermont. He was about twenty-six years of age and dedicated to becoming a top chef in the inn and hotel business. As far as I was concerned he had already arrived in the art of preparing scallops. Delicious! The only restriction on his schedule was that he could not leave until after the breakfast hour.

D on Abbott, above, runs a taxi service in Lee, Massachusetts, where he had grown up on a farm. His step-parents farmed 300 acres and had some thirty-five head of cattle. When the shift to machine-farming came, his parents could not make the needed investment; so farming could not provide a living. Don decided to go into the Army. His parents told him that the Army wouldn't take a farmer's boy. But it did.

He went through the Second World War without getting injured, but in 1964, he lost a leg. A backhoe turned over on him and one of its fins hacked off his leg. He had lain pinned under the machine for over an hour until the waterboy came along. It was 10° Fahrenheit. They sewed the leg back on, but gangrene had set in.

He had a hard time adjusting to $100 a week after $300 a week. He said that he became a common drunk for a time. His wife almost left him, but he and she finally adjusted.

We needed only two and one-half days to complete the Trail in New York state. So, even though the weekend weather forecast was for scattered showers, we decided to go ahead and keep our reservation for a motel room at Pine Grove Motel in Poughquag, run by Mrs. Ralph Pagano (Jane), who had said that she or her husband would provide shuttle service for us during the weekend. We started hiking the next morning, Saturday, and since it was raining, we made good time; there were no temptations to take long rest breaks.

During the afternoon a young backpacker overtook us. Tah recognized the insignia on his tee-shirt and commented that we seemed to see a lot of those on the Trail. "Why?" We discovered that his was the only one we had seen. It turned out that we had met him at Delaware Water Gap the prior Sunday. During the week he had hiked from the Gap across New Jersey and to Pawling, New York, averaging twenty-five miles a day. His hike had started three weeks earlier at Harpers Ferry and was terminating with a train ride home from Pawling.

While we waited for Jane to come to pick us up, another backpacker arrived and he and our newly-found friend greeted each other gustily. They had been hiking together for a couple of weeks and had thought they had said "Good-bye" for the summer. It turned out that those two were together when we had met at Delaware Water Gap. He confirmed the meeting by asking Tah if she still smoked a pipe!

Jane and Ralph Pagano had bought the Pine Grove Motel three and one-half years earlier as their place of retirement. Ralph had a goal of retiring at age fifty-five, just two and one-half years away.

Jane ran the motel while Ralph commuted daily to the Bronx in New York City (about an hour and a half in driving time one-way), where he was the night manager of a very profitable motel. It was a 27-unit motel, but earnings for a twenty-four hour period were more than Ralph and Jane's motel earned in a week. Ralph said that he was held up fourteen times by robbers during the years he worked at the Bronx motel. He had a gun hidden somewhere in the office and said he would use it to foil an attempted robbery if he ever had the advantage. "The people and the type of business being done at Pine Grove Motel compared to the Bronx motel is like being in another world," he said.

Ralph and Jane did all their own work. They planned to add ten efficiency apartments to the five they already had and rent them by the month. This type of business isn't too profitable, but it helps to carry them over the slow months.

We backpacked from Highway 9 (Bennington, Vermont) to Route 11 (Bromley) in four days, a leisurely October trek. The second night out, we stayed at the Caughnawaga Shelter. We shared the evening pleasantly with Alex from Maryland. He said that he did not know whether he would hike the entire Trail. For the present he was trying to think through some personal problems while hiking for a few days. To make a living, he bought old barns, tore them down and salvaged the old timbers and planks to sell into a market hungry for that kind of material.

The third night out, we stopped at one of the Bourn Pond Shelters. There we had the company of three Forest Service workers, who were in the midst of relocating the Trail and moving the shelters out of the recently designated wilderness area.

This was the message, a combination Irish blessing and Irish toast, which John Collins wrote in the log book at the Hurd Brook Lean-to:

"May the road rise to meet you;
May the wind always be at your back.
May the sun shine warm upon your face
And the rains fall soft upon your fields.
Until we meet again, may God hold you in the
    hollow of his hand.
May you be in heaven a half hour before the devil
    knows you're dead."

This was the last lean-to a hiker stays in before reaching Katahdin Stream Campground as he travels north on the northernmost section of the Appalachian Trail in Maine. John had only two more days of hiking to reach the end of the Trail, the top of Katahdin, an objective he had established earlier in the year when he had set out from Springer Mountain. As of September 10, after five months of backpacking, he had to hike the Trail in Virginia and the rest of Maine to complete the full 2,100 miles. He had saved Virginia for the last because it is near home in Washington, D.C.

We first saw John as he came out of the woods to the Hurd Brook Lean-to, where we had settled in for our 13th night on the 100-mile wilderness section of the Appalachian Trail between Monson and Abol Bridge, Maine. John called out as he arrived, "Well, you have settled it for me; I'll stop here for the night instead of going on to Abol Bridge. May I share the warmth of your fire?"

We were glad to have friendly company. His conviviality added a great deal of warmth to the cool night, as he talked freely of his family, himself, and the hundreds of people he had met on the Trail. He had retired at age sixty-two in March. He had been a sheet-metal worker in the construction industry. He had set a goal of hiking the Trail in 1975, after which he wanted to take up cross-country skiing. That's what he thinks retirement is all about, doing the things he'd always wanted to do. He had always wanted to hike the Appalachian Trail with his wife. But on the practice hikes she had discovered that hiking was not her sport; she did not quite

218

understand why John wanted to climb every hill he saw. So she stayed home. From time to time she mailed food to him. He explained that the fancy, freeze-dried foods came from the wife; he would never buy them for himself; he was too "economical minded." He said that he was one of ten children in a "one roller-skate family." The parents were Irish Catholic immigrants. John and his wife have five children.

John was hiking in a checkered wool woodsman's shirt and a pair of olive walking shorts which he had repaired with nylon thread. There was hardly a three-inch square area which had not been ripped and repaired. At night he pulled on a moth-eaten sweater which his wife had tried to talk him into discarding. He said that he was willing if she replaced it with a Cashmere sweater the equal of the one he was wearing.

As it got dark we went to bed in our sleeping bags in the lean-to. Then John began an hour-long songfest during which he sang at least twenty old popular tunes, mostly Irish.

During our stay at the Hurd Brook Lean-to, we met two young men, each about nineteen and each on his first extended hike. The first one was already there as we arrived. He had found the lean-to in a terrible mess and at around noon he had set about cleaning the place up. He had spent two hours at the task and was about ready to move on to the Rainbow Ledges to spend the night. We guessed that he was disillusioned by the messy condition of his first lean-to. We had read in the earlier logs along the way about the terrible condition of the Hurd Brook Lean-to. Our young friend had improved its appearance considerably.

The second nineteen-year-old came in to spend the night. His name was Ed Feeley and he was from a small town in southern Massachusetts near the Rhode Island line. He was reacting to an unexpected turndown by the Merchant Marine Academy. He had been accepted during the summer based upon his application and high school credits. However, when he showed up for admission in late August, he flunked the eye examination.

Ed spoke only occasionally, seemingly awed by John. At one point John asked him to sing but he declined, saying that he did not know the old songs. He knew the modern rock songs which were not a part of John's repertoire.

The three hikers whom we met at Hurd were hiking as singles.

During the busy season of May through September, hiking alone may be all right because there is a lot of traffic. We have found that the more general practice is for hikers to travel in pairs or even in groups. Most through-hikers were in their late teens to late twenties. We, John Collins, an eighty-six year old man who completed the Trail in 1975 and the seventy-six year old woman who hiked it in both directions are unusual cases.

Chuck was a mid-thirty-year-old bachelor living in an old farm house in the country near Clarendon, Vermont. His house was right on the Appalachian Trail (or Long Trail as it is known in those parts) where it crosses Route 103. Chuck had unofficially adopted two teenage boys whose single parents were in such desperate straits that they were happy for them to find this home. When the adoption papers become official, the seventeen and thirteen year-olds would change their family names to match Chuck's. They had already started calling Chuck, "Dad."

Chuck had a contract with the county to deliver school bus service from his area to Clarendon. The two boys rode the bus to and from school. Before and after school, on weekends and during vacations, they had chores helping Chuck around the place. They helped organize and run horse and pony shows on Saturdays in their private ring on the premises.

Chuck was glad to drive us to our entry point in East Wallingford and to park our car at his house for us to pick up later. He would not accept any pay at first, but we pressed him to take ten dollars to invest in something for the boys. He accepted it.

Of those whom we met, the couple who came the farthest distance to hike the Trail were Don and Balbi from Hawaii. Don was originally from Memphis, Tennessee and as a Marine had been stationed in Hawaii, where he met Balbi. When his service commitment was over, he had stayed to go to college and had majored in political science. We met Don and Balbi at the Speck Pond

Shelter (southwest Maine) at which we had arrived about two p.m., after climbing and descending Old Speck Mountain north to south.

The shelter was the regular three-sided enclosure; but it was surrounded by several tent platforms, which indicated a fairly heavy use during season. These platforms were built of sawed wood and timbers, providing a smooth, raised area on which tents could be erected. During season Speck and other shelter sites in this area were tended by a manager in residence who assigned platforms or places to sleep for a nominal fee.

As I was collecting wood for a fire, Don and Balbi arrived from the south. They had just completed Mahoosuc Notch and they looked a bit weary. They also appeared to be somewhat non-communicative with each other. In the course of our conversation, we wanted to know about the Notch which we were to tackle the next day. Is it really all that tough? "Oh, well, it is difficult," Don said; "but I could have done it much faster if Balbi could have kept up."

Balbi spoke up, "There were places where I was not strong enough to climb the boulders with my pack on. And I would recommend resting frequently as you go through."

We told them that if it took a couple of 26-year-olds like them two hours, it would take us twice that or four hours. Naturally I did not believe that we would really take four hours to walk one mile. As it turned out it took us three hours!

Don and Balbi had lunch and then decided not to try to go across Old Speck that day. They had sent their tent home when they reached the Presidentials and did not want to risk having to sleep out on the Trail in such uncertain weather.

Almost as soon as they made the decision not to hike the rest of the day, their tensions seemed to relax. They became pleasantly communicative from then on.

They had three weeks to go 270 miles to complete the Trail at Katahdin before the mountain's closing date of October 15. Beyond Grafton Notch or Old Speck Mountain, the Trail was comparatively easy and they could log several twenty-mile days. Furthermore they had the option of hitching from Monson to Baxter State Park and hiking south from Katahdin the last 114 miles. So they did not have to be tense.

222

"Goose" Gosnell (above), the policeman in Hot Springs, North Carolina, assured us that he normally would have been glad to shuttle us to Allen Gap and return with our car to Hot Springs. However, he couldn't because he had to stay close to the middle of town on election day. Instead, "Goose" arranged for Robert Shelton to shuttle us. Robert had relatives at Sams Gap (see page 19).

At Gentian Pond Shelter, the last shelter in New Hampshire going north, were Fred and "Tennis Shoe" Barb. We had first met Fred down in Virginia on the relocated trail on North Mountain. In real life, he was a writer for a Wall Street letter. He was hiking the Trail to "start over," to avoid being dead by age thirty. He said, "I used to be a normal human being, had a good-paying job, wore suits and ties, ate steaks, and paid rent." On the Trail he wore a beard, ate grains and no meat, had lost forty pounds, down to 160. "I have a complete change in lifestyle and will never go back to the old way."

"Tennis Shoe" Barb was an ex-competitive swimmer from Michigan. She was a good-looking Amazon carrying a fifty-pound pack and wearing tennis shoes instead of boots. To that point she had worn out four pairs and would expect the current pair to last to Katahdin.

Tah and I are grateful that the slender roots which our family has in New England are being nurtured and refreshed by our dear friends, the Drews. We enjoy hiking in New England during the foliage season, around Columbus Day weekend, winding up in Vershire, Vermont, with the Drews to celebrate Tah's birthday on October 10. Often, Ben and Sally Drew join us in a "celebration hike" on the AT.

We kinda grew into maturity with the Drews, after we moved into Westford, Massachusetts over thirty years ago. We lived next door to the Drew Fruit Farm. That's where Ben and Sally and their five children lived, worked, and played. They were a stable, first family in the community. Ben was the major apple grower in the area. He was an astute businessman and a leader in community affairs. He was the town moderator, having responsibility for chairing all town meetings.

Sally carried her community volunteer responsibilities with grace and charm, while caring for her brood of five. Her forebears had bequeathed substantial holdings in manufacturing and real estate companies, which required a considerable amount of her and Ben's time and attention.

When the Drew children had grown up, Sal felt a strong urge to develop a professional capability which was needed and wanted enough for someone to pay for her services. She had concluded that however noble volunteer work is, as long as it's for free, there's less than full dedication on the part of the volunteer and less than full appreciation on the part of the agency or the citizens. So she studied library science, became a fully qualified librarian and took a paying job as a librarian in Boston, to which she commuted. At last she felt professionally appreciated because she was paid for "volunteer work"!

Looking back upon the Westford days, Tah recalls that the nine children of both families added the spice of life to our friendship with the Drews. She feels that Sally gave her the needed support to do the more unusual adventures. The two of them took five children from both families (ages ten to fifteen) in a Volkswagen bus on a six-week tour through Europe. Then they took three older children for a three-week horse-back trip through Vermont. One summer they rented a summer cottage in Goose Rocks, Maine, hired two highschool girls and spent the summer on the beach with their eight children. (Our fourth had not yet been born.) Ben and I went to the cottage on weekends. It was a "jumping" house, overflowing with kids, ages two to fourteen, and their various friends. We marvelled at collected shells, carefully made sandcastles, ate the snails saved for us by the children, took rides in the boats rowed by the older children, and watched with mixed emotions as Rennie (the oldest Drew boy) affixed his father's pajama bottoms as a sail on the row boat. At night we fell into beds, exhausted, only to find that the beds had been wetted and sanded by the two and three-year olds who insisted on taking naps in daddy's bed. Those were exhilarating weekends; it was a relief to get back into the calm of the office on Monday morning!

It was natural that when Ben and Sal made a plan for retirement, they looked for some acreage in Vermont with at least two qualifications: the land should be suitable for Ben to develop for apple growing and the location should be near Hanover, New Hampshire the site of Dartmouth College, Ben's alma mater.

We look forward to future New England hikes on the Appalachian Trail with our friends, the Drews.

In Retrospect

From the tops of most ridges and balds of the Appalachian Range, one can see fold upon fold of mountains. Most notable in my recollection are the views of ridges "rolling into seeming infinity" from the peak of Standing Indian, the "Grandstand of the Southern Appalachians," and the extraordinary grandeur of the Smokies and the Pisgah from all points of outlook.

These rolling views are repeated from the top of Roan Mountain in the Cherokee in Tennessee and again and again from the peaks and ridges of the White Mountains in New Hampshire. Then in the Mahoosucs of northeast New Hampshire and southwest Maine, the views of the Presidentials are repeatedly rewarding. They are not dramatic or exciting as rugged mountains, but these ancient White Mountains are consoling and reassuring. I am confident that those who live at the feet of those mountains look to them for the source of their strength.

But perhaps the most rewarding of all outlooks came in Maine when we reached the Myron H. Avery Peak in the Bigelow Range. As the rain clouds lifted and the mists dissolved, we looked to the northeast. And there across the immense expanse of the lake country wilderness we looked upon Katahdin. It was magnificent. It's only one mile high above sea level but it rises out of the surrounding plains almost all of its full stature.

We came to respect Katahdin perhaps more than any other single mountain. Maybe we did because it is the goal of all Appalachian Trail hikers departing from Georgia. It caught our fancy and attention.

The majesty of the mountains and the wildernesses, the fullness of the autumn foliage colors, the blooms and births of nature in spring and the joys of being a part of it all bring tears to the contemplative soul. We are grateful for having had the opportunity to share in it.

—BEAVER BROOK TRAIL—
TO CASCADES   0.3
ASQUAM-RIDGE TR 1.6
SUMMIT   3.2
HANOVER, NH   49.9
BARNARD GULF, VT 70.6

THIS TRAIL IS EXTREMELY
ROUGH. IF YOU LACK EX-
PERIENCE, PLEASE USE AN-
OTHER TRAIL. TAKE SPECIAL
CARE AT THE CASCADES
TO AVOID TRAGIC RESULTS

Appendix

The remarkable story of a remarkable American institution, a 2,100-mile footpath, is told in *The Appalachian Trail Conference Member Handbook.* Chapter 8, "History of the Appalachian Trail," summarizes the fifty-plus years of Trail history, beginning with Benton MacKaye's proposal for the AT in 1921 to the 22nd annual meeting of the Conference in Carrabassett, Maine, 1979.

An interesting statement in this publication is that although the Trail's development "might be expected to follow the organization of interested groups in the regions through which it passed, in fact the exact reverse has occurred. The Trail has gone first; the clubs have followed in its wake."

There were no mountaineering organizations south of New York in the eastern part of the United States prior to 1924. Then came the Smoky Mountains Hiking Club of Knoxville. And gradually as the Trail was pushed farther south, clubs sprang up all along its route. Today there are sixty-three hiking or outing clubs, thirty-five of which carry responsibility for maintaining sections of the Trail, ranging from 5 miles of Trail for the York, Pennsylvania hiking club to the 277 miles maintained by the Maine AT club.

TRAIL MAINTAINING ORGANIZATIONS

Organization	Section Maintained	Miles
Maine Appalachian Trail Club	Katahdin summit to Maine Hwy. 26	277.1
Appalachian Mountain Club	Maine Hwy. 26 to Maine-N.H. Line	14.4
Appalachian Mountain Club	Maine-N.H. Line to Kinsman Notch	98.96
Dartmouth Outing Club	Kinsman Notch to N.H.-Vt. Line	49.24
Dartmouth Outing Club	N.H. Line to Vt. Hwy. 12	20.76
Green Mountain Club	Vt. Hwy. 12 to Vt.-Mass. Line	115.7
AMC Berkshire Chapter	Vt.-Mass. Line to Mass.-Conn. Line	84.2
AMC Connecticut Chapter	Mass.-Conn. Line to Conn. N.Y. Line	56.1
New York-New Jersey Trail Conference	Conn.-N.Y. Line to Delaware Water Gap	157.6
Springfield Trail Club	Delaware Water Gap to Fox Gap	7.2
Back to Nature Hiking Club	Fox Gap to Wind Gap	8.7
AMC Del. Valley Chapter	Wind Gap to Little Gap	15.9
Philadelphia Trail Club	Little Gap to Lehigh Furnace Gap	10.5
Blue Mtn. Eagle Climbing Club	Lehigh Furnace Gap to Bake Oven Knob	62.0
	Tri-County Corner to Rausch Creek	
Allentown Hiking Club	Bake Oven Knob to Tri-County Corner	11.3
Brandywine Valley Outing Club	Rausch Creek to Pa. Hwy. 325	13.6
Susquehanna A.T. Club	Pa. Hwy. 325 to Pa Hwy. 225	9.2
York Hiking Club	Pa. Hwy 225 to Susquehanna River	5.0
Mountain Club of Maryland	Susquehanna River to Pine Grove Furnace	45.9
Potomac Appalachian Trail Club	Pine Grove Furnace to Pa.-Md. Line	35.1
Potomac Appalachian Trail Club	Pa.-Md. Line to Potomac River	39.7

232

Potomac Appalachian Trail Club	Potomac River to Rockfish Gap	153.8
Old Dominion A.T. Club	Rockfish Gap to Reeds Gap	22.7
Tidewater A.T. Club	Reeds Gap to Tye River	9.8
Natural Bridge A.T. Club	Tye River to Black Horse Gap	86.1
Roanoke A.T. Club	Black Horse Gap to Crandon	136.3
Kanawha Trail Club	Stoney Creek to New River	17.7
Virginia Tech Outing Club	Crandon to Big Walker Lookout	21.6
Piedmont A.T. Club	Big Walker Lookout to Va. Hwy. 16	26.5
Mt. Rogers A.T. Club	Va. Hwy. 16 to Va.-Tn. Line	55.6
Tennessee Eastman Hiking Club	Va.-Tn. Line to Spivey Gap	116.2
Carolina Mountain Club	Spivey Gap to Big Pigeon River	85.5
Smoky Mountain Hiking Club	Big Pigeon River to Nantahala River	98.9
Nantahala Hiking Club	Nantahala River to N.C.-Ga Line	54.6
Georgia A.T. Club	N.C.-Ga. Line to Springer Mountain	79.1
Total		2102.56

All praises should be sung to all sixty-three clubs, whose members volunteer to preserve and maintain the Trail! We had the pleasure of seeing some of the volunteers in action on weekends. A member of the Potomac ATC arrived early at the entrance of the section which we planned to hike one Saturday morning in northern Virginia. He had with him a pair of heavy duty clippers and he was bidding "good-day" to his wife who had driven him to the entrance point. To have arrrived that early, after two hours of driving from Washington, D.C., they had to have left before daybreak. He appeared to be as happy to start clipping weeds and vines as we were to start walking. And his target for the weekend was about six miles of trail.

On another occasion, as we came off Mt. Moosilauke in early fall in New Hampshire, we recognized that we were in DOC or Dartmouth Outing Club country. A young man was grooming the

Trail. He was pegging small logs diagonally across the Trail to direct water off into the woods to prevent washouts and erosion. He told us that he was a freshman merely carrying out the initiating ritual of joining the DOC. We thoroughly enjoyed the seventy-five miles of DOC-maintained trail between Vermont Route 12 and Kinsman Notch, New Hampshire.

The length of the Appalachian Trail varies year to year, generally getting longer as relocations occur. The Appalachian Trail Data Book (1979) lists the length as 2,102.56. Since that publication date there have been relocations in southwest Virginia which added several miles. It's a rare occasion when a relocation does not add miles. We call it 2,100 miles as a round number. Even this does not take into account the many miles we hiked getting into and off the Trail when we had impassable lead-in roads.

A tabulation of our hiking shows:

Total Miles Hiked	2,100
Days hiked	244
Average miles per day	8.6
Backpack miles	545
Percentage of total	26%
Backpack days	71
Percentage of total	29%

Miles hiked in Season of Year and Percentage		
Spring	903 miles	43%
Summer	63 miles	3%
Fall	1,134 miles	54%
	2,100 miles	100%

Miles per day are a poor measure of the difficulty of the hike. Hours per day provide a somewhat better measure, but even the statement of hours cannot adequately describe the degree of difficulty. Something has to be said about the terrain in connection with the miles and hours. Of course, a statement of either miles or hours in the extreme can be very descriptive, such as a thirty-mile day or an eighteen-hour hike. Such hikes are tiring or exhausting regardless of terrain.

An eight-hour hike of only five miles from Speck Pond Shelter to Full Goose Shelter in Maine is a demanding day, as anyone who has done it will attest. Part of this hike requires traversing the Mahoosuc Notch, which is only one mile long and is practically level. It is a gorge lying between two sharply rising, cliff-like mountains whose walls have tumbled large boulders into the Notch. The traversing, with backpack, is tortuous, in many spots requiring scrambling over challenging ten-foot high boulders or crawling through narrow, cave-like openings, dragging the backpack along. It takes strength, stamina and patience. And then, immediately after emerging from the south end of the Notch, the north-to-south hiker has to climb a mountain on a trail devoid of switchbacks. It's no exaggeration to say that one could have hiked a twenty-mile day of normal hilly terrain and not have exerted any more energy!

We rarely hiked more than eight hours or more than fifteen miles a day. Our average of 8.6 miles a day is fairly representative. The 244 days included every day that we hiked, whether it was for one and a half hours, twelve hours, three miles or sixteen miles. If we hiked at all on the Trail, we counted the day. Quite frequently we vowed never to do any double-digit (hours or miles) hiking again. We seldomly remembered the vows!

We made no attempt to keep track of our expenses related to hiking. If we had, I suspect that we could claim a new record for cost-per-mile of hiking. When we were not backpacking, we searched out a good motel or guest room in the vicinity of a series of day hikes. We enjoyed dining out, particularly in New England at the old inns. We especially like Hanover Inn, Hanover, N.H.; Hartness Inn, Springfield, Vt.; Norwich Inn, Norwich, Vt.; Kedron Valley Inn, South Woodstock, Vt.; and in Virginia, Big Meadows in the Shenandoah National Park and Wayside Inn, Middletown. We also liked to get established for several days at a time, being willing to drive twenty to thirty miles on either side of our quarters to do day hikes. This permitted us to unpack and explore the region at leisure after the daily hike was over. Oftentimes we finished hiking by noon or shortly thereafter. To do this we tried to get started at daybreak. Then the afternoons and early evenings were free for exploring. However, we didn't learn much after dark. We went to bed quite early.